CONVICTED OF MURDER AND ABDU̲C̲T̲I̲O̲N̲ ̲C̲H̲E̲N̲E̲

"Based on the True Story of the Abduction & Murder

Of Victoria Stafford Canada's Angel".

By Dianna Holden

CHAPTER 1
"The Beginning"

April 8, 2009

It was a school day in the city of Woodstock, Ontario, Canada. The snow was just about dispersed as all traces of winter were about to disappear. Farmers were unable to start farming because the ground still had a centimeter of snow on it which melted in the latter part of the day. The temperature was a brisk -2.5. Today was anything but an ordinary one for 8 year old Victoria Stafford.

This was the first week that she was in her new house as her family had moved the week before. This was the day that would become a part of the history of Woodstock, but not in a positive way. You see this is the day that Victoria Stafford was abducted while walking home from her elementary school.

At 3:30 pm the clanging of the elementary school bell of Oliver Stephens Public School could be heard in the distance, signaling the end of the school day.

It was at this bell that according to various media reports that 8 year old Victoria walked away from her

Elementary school, with an unidentified female, that was wearing a puffy white coat.

The true events that occurred during the abduction of Miss. Stafford are only known by the individual(s) that are truly responsible for her abduction, however media reports have stated that Miss. Stafford was last seen on a surveillance tape at 3:32 pm walking with a women who was approximately 5 foot 1, weighing 115 to 120 lbs, wearing a white puffy winter coat, black jeans, with long dark hair pulled neatly back in a ponytail.

It is alleged that police were initially contacted at approximately 6:36 pm; three hours after Victoria first went missing. As to who specifically made the missing persons report and as to why there was such a delay is unknown.

During the evening of Victoria's disappearance there were many different theories with respect to the actions of the birth mother and the step father of Miss. Stafford. It was alleged that Mr. Goris took a three hour shower which is why he allegedly wasn't assisting with the search early on for Victoria, it was alleged that Ms. McDonald was sleeping. Many theories were stated but nothing substantiated, only Ms. McDonald & Mr. Goris knew what they were doing at the time Miss. Stafford was abducted from her school.

The fact remained regardless of speculation an 8 year old girl was missing, and needed to be found, regardless of the reason behind her disappearance. The mere thought that an innocent child could go missing, from a community with the population of only thirty-two thousand, a community where it's said that "**everyone knows everyone**" was a huge reality check for parents and citizens of Woodstock.

Victoria's disappearance was the beginning of a nightmare for all those involved and citizens alike. Strangers, banded together, holding candle light vigils, opening chat groups on Social Networking Sites, such as Facebook, to help find Canada's little angel.

Meanwhile, the nightmare of the ordeal began to unravel when police released an enhanced version of the surveillance video of Miss. Stafford walking away, with what appeared to be by her own free will, with an unidentified woman in a puffy white coat, with dark brown hair, which was slicked back in a tight ponytail.

It was at this time that the real speculations commenced both in the city of Woodstock itself, as well as online, and within the media.

CHAPTER 2

"The Media"

Often when we think of the media we think of newspapers, and television. We think of the people who put the news out there to keep us informed of what has happened in the world. Some people like the media, and others do not. However the media plays a very important role in society, and for Victoria Stafford, the media was her best friend, and her advocate, essentially the media became her voice.

Knowing that your daughter is missing is one thing, going to the media, is a decision that is very difficult to make for some people, because there is always the stereo-typical concern that the media may change what you say, present what you say in such a way that it's taken out of context. When it's a situation where you need to get your daughters photo and story out there, it's the fastest way to gain that attention that is much needed for missing person's cases. So it can only be imagined that, that was the reasons that Ms. McDonald decided to hold daily press conferences, to help find her daughter.

As the press conferences continued it would become apparent that perhaps this may have been the continued need for the press. It was like there was a major thirst for the media to know every little detail of Ms. McDonalds life, even if one conference would conflict with other stories she provided the media.

Each conference had to be much better than the previous, that much more dramatic then the next one. It became apparent that, for some who followed the Stafford case in the media, it was starting to get better than any made for Hollywood Movie, as the story had all the elements, from an alleged drug debt, to a mysterious limo ride to Toronto to meet a wealthy benefactor, to the alleged gang involvement. This case had it all.

The media did a wonderful job with the daily pressers, considering there were not many developments, on a daily basis. Through the camera lenses society was able to be kept up to date with the latest developments of the

Stafford Case, but also provided many the opportunities to see firsthand Ms. McDonald's pleas to locate her daughter.

The media also picked up numerous inconsistencies with Ms. McDonald's story, now whether or not the inconsistencies were caused by an actual change of story by Ms. McDonald or if it was just the reporters whom were trying to add their own spice to the story that reflected the inconsistencies, the fact remains the newspaper articles made it appear that Ms. McDonald was being less than honest to the cameras.

With the way the media presented the Stafford Case, it appears that this may have been what started the speculations on the internet and throughout the town of Woodstock Ontario, of the mother and stepfather being involved in such a horrendous crime.

In retrospect, it may have been better if Ms. McDonald stayed out of the media eye or perhaps had an agent to speak to the media, because every time she opened her mouth, speculations started stirring, regardless if she was being honest or not, the media had already damaged her.

Ms. McDonald really didn't portray herself as a grieving mother, not stating she wasn't grieving her loss, but the lack of visible emotion was almost unheard of in cases where a child is missing, then abducted and murdered. Throughout all the media reports, Ms. McDonald came across as a mother who just didn't care; she didn't have the emotion that is considered "typical", of a grieving mother.

Truly, how does a mother react to such a horrific situation? Here you are a mother of a beautiful daughter whom you allow to go to school and walk home for the first time by themselves, because you feel that they are responsible enough. You feel, as their mother that it is a safe neighborhood. And then all of a sudden the unimaginable occurs. Your daughter doesn't arrive home when she is supposed to.

You want to think the best; oh she's just visiting a friend, or hanging out. When do you decide to call the police? Do you call right away, only to find out that oh she's fine? Do you start the search yourself and then after three hours call the police because now you know that your daughter is missing.

In Ms. McDonald's case for whatever reason police were not notified for over three hours, after Miss. Stafford left the school. The extensive delay made it much more difficult for Law Enforcement to conduct their search, as three hours after a person goes missing is quite a lot of time before commencing a search for an adult let alone a small child.

Although there was a delay in reporting to police that Miss Stafford was missing, the police utilized as much of their resources that they possibly had, by midnight, they had notified the surrounding jurisdictions, to help assist locating Miss. Stafford.

One of the main resources which was utilized in this case was the media, both television, print and the internet.

On April 12, 2009, Ms. McDonald held her first press conference under the public eye at a candle light vigil in the Zellers Parking Lot, in Brantford.

This was the beginning of the press conferences, to help find Miss. Stafford. During the press conferences that were held at Ms. McDonalds house, a large number of inconsistencies started to occur, whether it was due to the way Ms. McDonald was portrayed in the media, or whether Ms. McDonald was deceiving the public, it is unclear. With the amount of different media outlets covering the story, it's no wonder there were fluctuations in the stories coming from anyone that was interviewed. Although, most of the discrepancies came from Ms. McDonald herself, there was the distinct possibility it occurred like that of someone playing the telephone game. You know where you say something by whispering in your friend's ear and they pass it down the line of about twenty or so people and the end result is never the same as what was initially said.

Due to all the inconsistent stories that were put out there in the media, it certainly made it extremely difficult for people in society to believe Ms. McDonald and to believe what actually happened did not have anything to do with the actions of Ms. McDonald or her common law partner, Mr. Goris.

One could only assume the media was correct, with what was put out there regarding this horrific case. As a member of society one only hopes that what they see in the news and read in the newspaper, that it is factual information and is not based on pure speculation.

Truly, the job of a newspaper reporter can be challenging at times, and perhaps with this case the media missed their mark, and neglected to assess how Ms. McDonald would be portrayed by the public. In reality many people in society began to form an opinion of Ms. McDonald, and the case itself as to who truly was ultimately responsible for the heinous act of Murder & Abduction.

The media portrayed the case as that of a made for Hollywood Movie; after all it had all the spicy elements of one. Was the way that the media portrayed the case to the general public skewed, by a thirst of wanting something new ahead of the competition at the daily news conferences, or was it actual fact. The answer is one of uncertainty. The elements of a Hollywood movie existed, from the mysterious limo ride to Toronto, to the possible gang involvement; to a possible psychic connection, it truly had all the makings of a movie. The elements that were presented changed the public's opinions rather quickly, for example when the media claimed that there may have been possible gang involvement or a drug debt people began to believe it.

Were these elements fact or were they fiction? Ms. McDonald claims she did go to

Toronto by Limo to a hotel to meet an unidentified person who wanted to help. The public was informed of this mysterious tale by the media who claimed it could have been a possible Mr. BIG sting by the police. The power of this suggestion led people to the assumptions that it was a definitive police sting that it couldn't actually have been the fact someone truly wanted to help.

The amount of media attention on this case was enormous, reporters were eating up the story and the sad part of the whole thing is so did the public. Hundreds of thousands of people focused their attention on their television sets, their radios, and to the internet to get whatever information they could about the case. People by the thousands were praying for a positive outcome.

The overwhelming response from the general public during such a crisis was absolutely astonishing with respect to this particular situation. Not only were people physically getting involved, to help find Canada's angel, but the chat rooms and forums of the Social Networking sites were lighting up like a Christmas tree.

CHAPTER 3

"Investigation Mishaps"

All along from the time that Miss. Stafford was reported missing, law enforcement agencies throughout the adjacent jurisdictions, and Woodstock itself were actively searching for her.

From the very beginning the search for Victoria Stafford was a difficult one. Although, a combination of law enforcement agencies, were conducting the search, law enforcement had to rely on good old door to door canvassing, and old fashioned police work, and the media and general public to help solve the disappearance of Miss. Stafford.

The police had a tough job on their hands; they were used to domestic assaults, drunk and disorderly conduct, giving out speeding tickets and other crimes, but they were not prepared for the murder and abduction of a small innocent child. The national murder rate in Woodstock, Ontario is 2 per 100,000 people; however with the population of 34 thousand, it makes the murder rate in Woodstock almost as dangerous as a large city such as Toronto, Ontario.

Needless to say with this type of murder rate, and such a small population, the police don't deal with abduction and murders on a regular basis in Woodstock, Ontario.

The police started their search by releasing an enhanced surveillance video of Victoria, walking away from the school with a woman. As they continued their search, with very little clues, they went door to door canvassing the neighborhood, checking cars, and fields. Their search didn't end with just door to door checks; they also checked dumpsters, and farmer's fields.

Law Enforcement Agencies throughout the country, were put on high alert, at airports, Victoria Stafford's photo was displayed, for everyone to see. Thousands of tips came into many different law enforcement agencies, which made the police investigation that more frustrating for detectives working the case.

Police personnel had a very large task on their hands, they had to weed out the tips which were reliable and which were not. What made matters worse was the internet social networking site, Facebook. Although Facebook became quite the tool for investigators whom were working the case, it also became a very dangerous site, as individuals were posting items of an evidentiary capacity, things that were only known to law enforcement agents close to the case.

Not only did this hinder the ongoing police investigation, but it created more work for the investigators, as now they had to track down who it was that posted, things, that should never have been known except to individuals that were directly involved in the case.

Many things that were kept out of the media, were being posted on Facebook, and the largest crime fighting website WEBSLOUTHS. This just made it that much more difficult for the investigation team to keep things under wrap.

The other big issue for Investigators regarding the internet discussion groups was that individuals would see a tip on the internet or something suspicious online and they would pick up the phone and call their local police, which clogged up the system with the same tips being reported over and over again. The online discussion groups that were talking about the Stafford Case also became a huge barrier to police as information was being leaked out online, and it also created major speculations in the case, which police had to follow up each and every post that may have had any relevance to the case. It was a daunting task, as many users on Facebook, especially those who were members of the variety of groups that discussed the Victoria Stafford case utilized fake accounts.

It was no easy job for the hundreds of investigators on the case. Emotions too ran high with many investigators in the case, this was no ordinary crime.

The pressure from the public and the media was astronomical, which put extra stress on the law enforcement agencies, to quickly wrap up the case and hold someone responsible. Law Enforcement had to prove to the public that the town of Woodstock was safe. That it wasn't ordinary that a child would go missing on their way home from school.

Investigators also had to provide an explanation as to why there was no "Amber" Alert called in this case.

The Amber Alert system is widely utilized with a missing child when there is a suspect description or vehicle to alert other general motorists that if they see it to call 911. In the Stafford case no Amber Alert was called because there was no named suspect, and no vehicle description. According to police it did not meet the Amber Alert Criteria.

Police in the case were criticized not only due to the Amber Alert not being called, but also because; the police did not deem Victoria's case as abduction. According to the surveillance video, police felt that Victoria was taken by someone whom she was familiar with, because stranger abductions are extremely rare.

From the very beginning of the case the Woodstock police department were not equipped to handle a case of such magnitude, and was pressured to put a close on this case.

On May 19, 2009 police made the arrest of 18 year old, Terri-Lynn Mcclintic, of Woodstock, and 29 year old Michael Rafferty.

Although arrests were made, it did not necessarily mean that 18 year old Mcclintic and 29 year old Rafferty were guilty of the offence.

Many people still believed that the birthmother and stepfather had to have had some involvement in the incident. However, without charges being laid against them, how could anyone continue to speculate their guilt? The forums on the social networking sites, Facebook, and web sleuths, lit up with all kinds of theories and speculations, as to what actually occurred on April the 8th. Considering all of the speculations and theories that continued after the arrests, it made it almost impossible for the Stafford and McDonald family to mourn their loss in private.

Media would pound on the doors, telephones would consistently ring, email messages and private messages would fly. All which made it emotionally draining on the combined families.

The police also had to attempt to keep under wraps the evidence in the case, although it was so difficult with everyone discussing the case via the World Wide Web. Could the police get a ban on the internet, to stop the mayhem that was occurring in the discussion forums about the case? Police would have loved to have a ban on everything that was stated on the internet however; in a new technological society it's almost impossible.

CHAPTER 4

"Question of Guilt"

Now what happens if you're a certain police detective, and you believe that one of the suspects you have in custody is innocent, but all kinds of threats are made, towards the suspects' life, and your higher-ups want to pin it on the suspect. What do you do then?

During the case a armchair detective, (slang for someone who was following the case) had a telephone conversation with a twenty year veteran of the Ontario Provincial Police. This certain armchair detective came to the opinion that the detective felt that the male accused Michael Rafferty was innocent in this case, and that the police knew this and made the arrests anyways. The OPP Detective, whom released this information, was it intentional as they wanted this information to get out in the public domain, or was in a slip up of investigation techniques while following up on information needed from civilians out there. Regardless, of why the discussion took place, it had and now it was putting this Armchair detective in an uncomfortable position.

To give you an idea as to why a possible police cover-up may have occurred in the Stafford Case here is the exclusive transcript of a conversation between an OPP Detective who was investigating the Stafford Case, and an individual whom followed the case from day one, who we will call for the sake of the conversation an armchair detective.

TRANSCRIPTION OF AUDIO TAPE

OPP DETECTIVE: It's (Name Deleted for privacy)

ARMCHAIR DETECTIVE: Oh hi sorry about that I was trying to call you back my phone was fucked.

OPP DETECTIVE: Yeah because you were trying to call me and you see I was trying to call you.

ARMCHAIR DETECTIVE: Laughs

OPP DETECTIVE: INAUDABLE Laughing

OPP DETECTIVE: So yeah No,

ARMCHAIR DETECTIVE: So my issue is simply this right because kay Tara McDonald had threatened a lot of people me being one of them. Okay

OPP DETECTIVE: uh huh

ARMCHAIR DETECTIVE: That she was going to sue me that she was going to you know to try to go to press charges

OPP DETECTIVE: why

ARMCHAIR DETECTIVE: Because of the fact that I was very bold with what I was typing on the internet about her. Okay the fact that I was discussing James Goris's previous allegations of Sexual Misconduct

OPP DETECTIVE: Yeah but

ARMCHAIR DETECTIVE: I didn't put any of that out there. Sorry I didn't really sleep well last night and I was going to talk to you

28

about it earlier this morning and I thought

no I'm like no I need to clear the air because

Im um kinda uncomfortable, and then what did

it for me

OPP DETECTIVE: Well

ARMCHAIR DETECTIVE: what did it for me

what finalized that was when I called your

number back I got some guy in electronic crime

and I'm like oh fuck .

OPP DETECTIVE: No you see when we're

working on a project, I'm sitting at another

desk, and you see right now I am doing whats

called key word searches on Michael Rafferty's

computer.

ARMCHAIR DETECTIVE: Yes

OPP DETECTIVE: So that's what I'm doing I

have to sit in electronic crime to do that.

ARMCHAIR DETECTIVE: I see

OPP DETECTIVE: So that's where my seat is so it has nothing to do with electronic crime.

ARMCHAIR DETECTIVE: Okay so then my other concern is that because as I mentioned yesterday Im pretty certain that Tara McDonald did this I'm concerned because there is a lot of gang activity involved in this I'm worried about my safety. If any of this comes out that I am giving you this information. Because ..

OPP DETECTIVE: No...

ARMCHAIR DETECTIVE: Kayla Hurst tends to sing like a bird, she couldn't keep her mouth shut worth shit And my concern is if I give you the recording of that conversation obviously your going to have to go back and talk to her after you hear the conversation right uhh my concern is she I don't know if she's friends with Tara McDonald Do you get what I'm saying.

OPP DETECTIVE: Yeah and you know well and I

ARMCHAIR DETECTIVE: And I have a family too that I need to protect as well. And …

ARMCHAIR DETECTIVE: And I do and I don't want to prevent justice from being served with Tara McDonald and or James Goris getting brought to justice on this but I am concerned for my safety as well.

OPP DETECTIVE: Well you know what basically what I want is that out of all of this

ARMCHAIR DETECTIVE: UM hum

OPP DETECTIVE: You hold the piece of the fact that Kayla lied to me at this point right now

ARMCHAIR DETECTIVE: UmHum

OPP DETECTIVE: that Kayla lied to me.

ARMCHAIR DETECTIVE: Okay

OPP DETECTIVE: So if she knows more… if she's getting information

ARMCHAIR DETECTIVE: Umhum

OPP DETECTIVE: Then we need to know that.

ARMCHAIR DETECTIVE: But then wouldn't you have that on Jail tapes if Terry-Lynn is actually talking to her

OPP DETECTIVE: No you see because that's what happens is you see we're not allowed to we have to get certain..

ARMCHAIR DETECTIVE: Warrants

OPP DETECTIVE: Warrants and stuff for jail house stuff because we cant just

ARMCHAIR DETECTIVE: Um huh

OPP DETECTIVE: tape a private conversations and

ARMCHAIR DETECTIVE: Okay

OPP DETECTIVE: Basically you see what happens is lots of times they don't do it because its too hard to turn it on and you cant turn them on and turn them off.

ARMCHAIR DETECTIVE: Yeah I know I hear ya

OPP DETECTIVE: inaudible Lawyer

ARMCHAIR DETECTIVE: Yeah

OPP DETECTIVE: and lots of times what happens is say she calls umm Carol

ARMCHAIR DETECTIVE: Yeap

OPP DETECTIVE: and maybe Carol puts her three way with a lawyer so you cant cause lots of times you cant get that.

ARMCHAIR DETECTIVE: Yeah I hear ya...

*OPP DETECTIVE: you know for that reason…
So I can tell you there is nothing in the jail
that allows us to see whos calling.*

*ARMCHAIR DETECTIVE: Yeah Well you see the
concern I have is because you and I both know
that Tara did this. And that James is
involved in this, and I guess my concern is
because I don't mind helping with respect to
bringing these people to justice, but because
I think that Victoria deserves justice but my
concern is that you know Tara McDonald had
threatened to sue me you know had was posting
things on board that she was going to get even
with me, you should see some the threats I
got, and that's my concern.*

OPP DETECTIVE: You see and that ----

*ARMCHAIR DETECTIVE: Shes scared and you
know damn right*

OPP DETECTIVE: Yeah and that is um that is all part and partial of this cause of what I'm afraid of is that there has been you know were not getting everything that we need.

ARMCHAIR DETECTIVE: What do you mean

OPP DETECTIVE: Well when I well Kayla is a prime example Kayla sat in there on Wednesday and said and oh no I was just kinda contacted and and all kinda simple and her big thing was that you portrayed yourself as a reporter, and wanted to talk to her about stuff.

ARMCHAIR DETECTIVE: I pertrayed myself to her as that I was writing a book

OPP DETECTIVE: Yeah

ARMCHAIR DETECTIVE: and that I wanted to talk to her and that's correct.

OPP DETECTIVE: But you see then, she said but I didn't know anything. I don't know anything then I said so why did she want to talk to you.

ARMCHAIR DETECTIVE: Umhum

OPP DETECTIVE: She made it look like it was there was no audio recording and that

ARMCHAIR DETECTIVE: So she Did you ask about the audio recording.

OPP DETECTIVE: yes

ARMCHAIR DETECTIVE: And she said there wasn't one

OPP DETECTIVE: She said that she wasn't that she didn't say yes to one then I asked her if she knew she was being audio taped, then she said there could be one because she saw it on facebook .because the whole facebook thing she was saying Carol got on her facebook account.

ARMCHAIR DETECTIVE: That's bullshit cause I talked to Kayla Hurst. But I don't think I'm gonna be completely frank I don't think that Kayla Hurst and Terry-Lynn have any contact. I don't. But Carol Mclintic you know and

ARMCHAIR DETECTIVE: You got to remember Carol Mclintic and Tara Mcdonald were doing drugs together

OPP DETECTIVE: Yeah

ARMCHAIR DETECTIVE: I do think that you guys have the wrong people still.

OPP DETECTIVE: And that's what we have to prove

ARMCHAIR DETECTIVE: Yeah and you think that too.

OPP DETECTIVE: Yeah and that's what we that's what we are looking for right now

ARMCHAIR DETECTIVE: So your trying to prove it Okay so whats going to happen if Tara and James get married?

OPP DETECTIVE: Um my understanding is that it isn't going to make any difference because it happened when they were not, but they probably don't know that.

ARMCHAIR DETECTIVE: Good

ARMCHAIR DETECTIVE: Good Their getting married Halloween Day but I haven't confirmed it s just the date ive been told.

OPP DETECTIVE: oh yeah well that's nice ...

ARMCHAIR DETECTIVE: Its not substantiated yet just to make it very clear its not substantiated but you know ...

OPP DETECTIVE: Well its Halloween (laughing)

ARMCHAIR DETECTIVE: Exactly

OPP DETECTIVE: Laughing

ARMCHAIR DETECTIVE: But you know.. How do I know kay question for you…for this.. the three pictures I have that are some what provacitive and pornographic   to speak of Tara Mcdonald how do I know who else has these photos

OPP DETECTIVE: Well you don't know

ARMCHAIR DETECTIVE: So if I give these to you..right which I think are crucial to your investigation of her umm how do I know that once she sees the photos that she doesn't know they came from me. As far as I know she doesn't even know that I have them.

OPP DETECTIVE: Well you know what well no no I don't think so because well I know for a fact that when I talked to this women

from Belville that they were on like
websleuths and

ARMCHAIR DETECTIVE: Yeah

OPP DETECTIVE: all the time

ARMCHAIR DETECTIVE: Be very careful
about websleuths because tara reads
everything that is on there.

OPP DETECTIVE: because there is all
kinds of people that are on there that
shouldn't be on there

Because this person saw the photos but
she didn't save them she didn't keep them.
She associated them with Tara trying to sell
something….

ARMCHAIR DETECTIVE: Well I thought that
she was trying to sell sex over the internet.
To be completely honest. That was my
impression of the photos.

OPP DETECTIVE: But there from how long ago…

ARMCHAIR DETECTIVE: they look recent they don't look very long ago I would say within (sigh) Fuck um No it would have been no she was skinny as friggen bones when this first happened, like she was skin and bones at the very beginning, and then she started bulking up because she didn't want to look like the police sketch, umm but I would say maybe I don't know how old she is see that is something that I didn't even look I would say shes about maybe in her mid twenties.

OPP DETECTIVE: Yeah

ARMCHAIR DETECTIVE: But you know You know about her other child don't you. Right? Other than Daryn

OPP DETECTIVE: No

ARMCHAIR DETECTIVE: You don't

OPP DETECTIVE: No I don't

ARMCHAIR DETECTIVE: She has another kid

OPP DETECTIVE: Okay …

ARMCHAIR DETECTIVE: If you look at the well I haven't sent it to you yet ….um on the conversation with Diane aka Rosie Smart,

OPP DETECTIVE: Yes

ARMCHAIR DETECTIVE: There are a whole wack of links in there look for the one because it has a picture of all of the kids. She has another child…

OPP DETECTIVE: Well where is that other child?

ARMCHAIR DETECTIVE: I don't know (PAUSE) I do not know and I believe it was another boy. And this isn't speculation this is fact and that's why I thought it was interesting that because when all the media reports everything Nobody mentioned this other child.

OPP DETECTIVE: No like I mean

ARMCHAIR DETECTIVE: Sorry I don't mean to floor you but

OPP DETECTIVE: Someone may know on our team but I know I don't know that because I have never been told that.

ARMCHAIR DETECTIVE: She does have another child. And the child wasn't an infant, he was either a couple years older than daryn or a couple years younger. Im not certain but there is another child. I am a hundred percent sure on that. Cause there is a picture of her and the other boys. And tori I believe wasn't in the photo. But there is another child.

OPP DETECTIVE: Hmmm

ARMCHAIR DETECTIVE: So I just thought well I meant to mention that to you yesterday but it slipped my mind.

OPP DETECTIVE: WOW…

ARMCHAIR DETECTIVE: Yeah and um yeah but there is definitely another child

OPP DETECTIVE: Wow

ARMCHAIR DETECTIVE: And you know but I guess I guess for safety reasons I don't want this women coming after me you know because she has been able to elude you this long… you know

OPP DETECTIVE: Yeah

ARMCHAIR DETECTIVE: That's my concern….
Like you know

OPP DETECTIVE: Well basically what I do like what I'm doing right now is writing up the report with my interview with Kayla and in turn I do a report of me talking to you to and then that's as far as it goes so I get it, the people that put it on our special computer system they get it,

ARMCHAIR DETECTIVE: Um Hum

OPP DETECTIVE: and that's it.

ARMCHAIR DETECTIVE: um hum

OPP DETECTIVE: All this is lots of the stuff we have received on this project

ARMCHAIR DETECTIVE: Um hum

OPP DETECTIVE: we use it as an investigative tool. So therefore its not disclosable.

ARMCHAIR DETECTIVE: Umhumm

OPP DETECTIVE: Because we all use it cause the stuff that you gave its investigative.

ARMCHAIR DETECTIVE: Umhumm.

OPP DETECTIVE: And what it is , is we track it down to the very end and then that's it.

ARMCHAIR DETECTIVE: Umhumm

OPP DETECTIVE: So that's why with Kayla I need to have something to say to say that you're a liar.

ARMCHAIR DETECTIVE: Well yeah she is a liar

OPP DETECTIVE: So then you know So thats

ARMCHAIR DETECTIVE: Yeah I know I hear ya.

ARMCHAIR DETECTIVE: But now what happens if once you go back to her what if she gets scared just hypothetically and starts talking to Tara?

OPP DETECTIVE: Kayla

ARMCHAIR DETECTIVE: Yeah because I still am uncertain as to what Kaylas involvement in all this is.

OPP DETECTIVE: See and I am I am the same because it's a whole drug thing

ARMCHAIR DETECTIVE: Yeah I know

OPP DETECTIVE: Umm Kaylas lied before …. so

ARMCHAIR DETECTIVE: Yeah but you know some of the things that she said rang some truth to it.

OPP DETECTIVE: Like what

ARMCHAIR DETECTIVE: Like little pieces like just little things just with respect to CAS

OPP DETECTIVE: Yeah like

ARMCHAIR DETECTIVE: Yeah with respect to the

OPP DETECTIVE: If you look at Kaylas facebook stuff there she has lots of pictures of her kids

ARMCHAIR DETECTIVE: Yeah

OPP DETECTIVE: But it doesn't say anywhere that she doesn't have her kids.

ARMCHAIR DETECTIVE: She doesn't have her kids, Kayla told me that she doesn't have her kids

OPP DETECTIVE: Why

ARMCHAIR DETECTIVE: She told me that Carol Mclintic was going to try to get her kids back for her. And she also said that um they were all adopted. Terry Lynn was adopted, umm I did some research into that as well and it was quite fascinating as to what I found out.

OPP DETECTIVE: Well you know but Kayla (unaudible)

ARMCHAIR DETECTIVE: Yeah but the sad thing about this is two innocent people are in jail. You know.

OPP DETECTIVE: Yeah

ARMCHAIR DETECTIVE: So what happens in cases like this you guys keep them in there until you get the right people?

OPP DETECTIVE: That's way above me (Laughing)

ARMCHAIR DETECTIVE: Have you ever seen this happen?

OPP DETECTIVE: NO , well I have never worked on anything like this in my life.

ARMCHAIR DETECTIVE: You've never seen it. (Laughing)

OPP DETECTIVE: Ive never Ive never seen anything like it

ARMCHAIR DETECTIVE: But they cant really let them out though because people would kill them.

OPP DETECTIVE: EXACTLY

ARMCHAIR DETECTIVE: you know even though their innocent. Like

OPP DETECTIVE: today on facebook they said that they've had to move Michael Raferty to Chatham

ARMCHAIR DETECTIVE: yeah I know

OPP DETECTIVE: To Chatham

ARMCHAIR DETECTIVE: yeah they have to move him because they're going to kill him.

OPP DETECTIVE: Yeah.

ARMCHAIR DETECTIVE: And I hope to god you guys are protecting him.

OPP DETECTIVE: So yeah its

ARMCHAIR DETECTIVE: You guys are going to have a huge law suit on your hands.

OPP DETECTIVE: Yeah!

ARMCHAIR DETECTIVE: But I am sure you guys can probably work out something

OPP DETECTIVE: Yeah

ARMCHAIR DETECTIVE: I just cant believe they jumped the gun on it but I can see why though look at the pressure...

OPP DETECTIVE: Yeah Yeah

ARMCHAIR DETECTIVE: you know

OPP DETECTIVE: It was the media attention the, fact that it was an eight year old yeah like it was there was hundreds and hundreds of investigators working on it 24/7.

ARMCHAIR DETECTIVE: Yeah I know I know...

ARMCHAIR DETECTIVE: But then whoever dropped the ball and said arrest this person their the one that is its all going to come down on.

OPP DETECTIVE: Yeah ….

ARMCHAIR DETECTIVE: I can see a whole bunch of people having to resign because of this…

OPP DETECTIVE: Inaudible

ARMCHAIR DETECTIVE: Sorry go ahead

OPP DETECTIVE: That's one good thing about me being at the lowest man on the totem pole

ARMCHAIR DETECTIVE: Laughs

OPP DETECTIVE: Laughs

OPP DETECTIVE: That I am just so insignificant that its like I'm the grunt

ARMCHAIR DETECTIVE: Just trying to make sure that the proper people get put

OPP DETECTIVE: You know what all I I have to cover all the bases

ARMCHAIR DETECTIVE: Yeah

OPP DETECTIVE: Im yeah I have to cover all the bases,

ARMCHAIR DETECTIVE: How long have you been a member ?

OPP DETECTIVE: Over 20 years

ARMCHAIR DETECTIVE: Wow and you have never seen something like this..

OPP DETECTIVE: NO I have never seen anything this huge before in my life.

ARMCHAIR DETECTIVE: Snickers

OPP DETECTIVE: and yeah I have worked on undercover stuff

ARMCHAIR DETECTIVE: yeah I hear ya

ARMCHAIR DETECTIVE: Was there connections between that Lorne Thomas

OPP DETECTIVE: That I haven't That I haven't verified yet.

ARMCHAIR DETECTIVE: You haven't seen it yet no because you know what I initially thought when I initially got involved in this was initially what I thought was it was a child selling ring.

OPP DETECTIVE: And Lots of people did....

ARMCHAIR DETECTIVE: And it makes sense

OPP DETECTIVE: Yeah

ARMCHAIR DETECTIVE: Because if you think about it you if you guys are able to get the dna from Roselyn Knecht, right and find out if she is actually that other one,

OPP DETECTIVE: Yeah

ARMCHAIR DETECTIVE: It makes perfect sense… there all together like they all know eachother and the fact that you know James Goris you know with its too bad that he was… you know got off on that thing because I …

OPP DETECTIVE: unaudible

ARMCHAIR DETECTIVE: because I believe he did it… and you know he just

OPP DETECTIVE: but that's what happens people say you know the child didn't want to testify you know well what their five theres not a more daunting task than to anything to do with court

ARMCHAIR DETECTIVE: um hmm

OPP DETECTIVE: I mean like kids just don't want to a Like I just had a case the other day where the adult did poorly on the stand

ARMCHAIR DETECTIVE: I hear ya…

OPP DETECTIVE: You know

ARMCHAIR DETECTIVE: Yeah its hard here we are today were sitting 5 months past Victoria Stafford being found, and theres still not been justice, yeah there are two people in custody, one that wants her fifteen minutes of fame

OPP DETECTIVE: Yeah

ARMCHAIR DETECTIVE: and the other one whos in there but shouldn't be. (giggle)

OPP DETECTIVE: Yeah I know I know uh Rafertty goes up for court today.

ARMCHAIR DETECTIVE: Okay

OPP DETECTIVE: So I don't know I haven't heard anything about what happened cause its just going to be all done through video.

ARMCHAIR DETECTIVE: Yeah but they cant let him out though because people will kill him

OPP DETECTIVE: no

ARMCHAIR DETECTIVE: So how do you guys protect him

OPP DETECTIVE: yeah

ARMCHAIR DETECTIVE: so what   cause they know that he is innocent, so how are they going to be able to drop the charges on something like this.

OPP DETECTIVE: Yeah like where do you go?

ARMCHAIR DETECTIVE: Well yeah that's what I'm saying So how can ya

OPP DETECTIVE: Yeah

ARMCHAIR DETECTIVE: what do you say? How can you You know what do you do.

OPP DETECTIVE: Say oh oh sorry yeah

ARMCHAIR DETECTIVE: Have you ever seen anything like this before ever.

OPP DETECTIVE: No NO

ARMCHAIR DETECTIVE: Do you think the Woodstock police just don't know how to drop the charges?

OPP DETECTIVE: Well I don't know if its that or I don't know if it's just I mean everything like the kinda information that is out there.

ARMCHAIR DETECTIVE: Umhmm

ARMCHAIR DETECTIVE: So basically usually what you guys like to see the saving graces and get the physical evidence against Tara and James You know what I was thinking, And I have a conversation that I had with Dianne you know Rosie Smart,

OPP DETECTIVE: Yeah

ARMCHAIR DETECTIVE: I didn't copy it because I wanted to tell you about it first you know IN a nutshell her and I were going to get together with some other people and email Tara

OPP DETECTIVE: Snickers

ARMCHAIR DETECTIVE: and say that we know that you did this and that we saw you do this and that you better go in and tell the police first and try to scare her into going to you without threats and stuff like that

Female 1 : Yeah Yeah

ARMCHAIR DETECTIVE: But if we do that can I get in shit? Laughs

OPP DETECTIVE: Nooo

ARMCHAIR DETECTIVE: Ok kay

OPP DETECTIVE: No

ARMCHAIR DETECTIVE: Because that's what we were going to do initially and see if she cracks….

OPP DETECTIVE: no cause because the I think its one of these where umm like especially in this day in age where everything being like worldwide

ARMCHAIR DETECTIVE: umhum

OPP DETECTIVE: like people like everyones out there. Like everybodys talking about it with everyone and um as far as like um like personally as far as you crossing the line like nobody has because she hasn't called anybody up and she hasn't called the police and said and reported you

ARMCHAIR DETECTIVE: Yeah ya

OPP DETECTIVE: You know what I mean

ARMCHAIR DETECTIVE: yep

OPP DETECTIVE: I think lots of times they just do lots of talk. And then just to say well

ARMCHAIR DETECTIVE: umhum

OPP DETECTIVE: Like you know

ARMCHAIR DETECTIVE: Yeah do you think shes get off on this

OPP DETECTIVE: I don't know you know what I don't know…

ARMCHAIR DETECTIVE: it makes me sick doesn't it you?

OPP DETECTIVE: Yeah Yeah

ARMCHAIR DETECTIVE: You know

ARMCHAIR DETECTIVE: Like I just um Did you guys do the like all the warrants for the cel phones.

OPP DETECTIVE: Yes

ARMCHAIR DETECTIVE: You did that all ready

OPP DETECTIVE: yeah weve got them all

ARMCHAIR DETECTIVE: ahh did you guys check Roselyn Knetchts cel phones

OPP DETECTIVE: that I don't know

ARMCHAIR DETECTIVE: You don't know….

Female 1: because that is a whole different

ARMCHAIR DETECTIVE: Somehow I think Roselyn Knecht and Sean Couch is involved in this ..

OPP DETECTIVE: well yeah you said the connection yesterday

ARMCHAIR DETECTIVE: Ya well ya

OPP DETECTIVE: yeah

ARMCHAIR DETECTIVE: But I don't know whats taking Edmonton so long Detective Antoniuk to go and do the you know to go and get the dna from her I guess if a person doesn't wna ot give dna to the police they don't have too

OPP DETECTIVE: Well yeah we're trying to establish a National database, to make it easier, for missing persons, it used to be the mother would just give dna. And just has it on file

Female2: it just frustrates me because I don't want to see her get off, I stopped researching for months but started again yesterday to try to find anything that you don't have and trying to establish the connection between her and rafferty, I still think Rafferty was honestly just an innocent pawn in this whole thing,

OPP DETECTIVE: And that very well could be... Yes that very well could be...

ARMCHAIR DETECTIVE: And that I just do and you know I think he probably borrowed leant his vehicle out. Did you happen to see the dog that was in the car

OPP DETECTIVE: Yeah I saw Yeah the dog yeah

ARMCHAIR DETECTIVE: You say that ok um ok cause that dog um its actually owned by James Goris,

OPP DETECTIVE: Oh is that who oh ok

ARMCHAIR DETECTIVE: does that help

OPP DETECTIVE: WOW

ARMCHAIR DETECTIVE: Like I told people that you fuck you could see aliens popping out of that if you look hard enough. Laughing

OPP DETECTIVE: Laughing

ARMCHAIR DETECTIVE: then I started looking at it but its snout was hangin over the seatbelt of the drivers side

OPP DETECTIVE: of the drivers side Yeah

ARMCHAIR DETECTIVE: So giggles its just

OPP DETECTIVE: How true giggles if you look at it long enough ooh yeah

ARMCHAIR DETECTIVE: laughing

OPP DETECTIVE: You look at it long enough its gonna move

ARMCHAIR DETECTIVE: Laughing.

OPP DETECTIVE: yeah I just saw that allright spending hours and hours of surveillance and like oh yeah I think I just saw something

ARMCHAIR DETECTIVE: yeah I know giggles Yeah I know

ARMCHAIR DETECTIVE: Yeah I'm in the process of getting my private investigation license.

OPP DETECTIVE: Oh Really

ARMCHAIR DETECTIVE: Yeah why I kinda draw a fine line on it laughs well that's why when you called me yesterday I thought I was being complained about again

OPP DETECTIVE: Oh

ARMCHAIR DETECTIVE: Well we lie when we call people and we say that someones been named on a will. Um and we need to get ahold of them.

OPP DETECTIVE: yeah and

ARMCHAIR DETECTIVE: I am really good we work a lot of Ontario Files a lot of shit out your way and so anyways so yeah uh I got complained on again so when you said Stafford I was like Oh, (Giggles)

OPP DETECTIVE: Giggles. No that wasn't it

ARMCHAIR DETECTIVE: So I was thinking ok Now what do I do..

OPP DETECTIVE: Yeah

ARMCHAIR DETECTIVE: So I

OPP DETECTIVE: So that's it if Tara had a huge issue with you as much as what she leads you to believe then she would have contacted us.

ARMCHAIR DETECTIVE: But then shes been threatening me through other things but I'm just concerned because of the fact that if James is involved with the Banditos like everyone is saying

OPP DETECTIVE: Well yeah of course yeah

ARMCHAIR DETECTIVE: That's my concern

OPP DETECTIVE: Well Absolutely

ARMCHAIR DETECTIVE: So you know if the gang it's a drug thing whatever its drugs so to speak

OPP DETECTIVE: Well Yeah

ARMCHAIR DETECTIVE: With the fact that James has a lot to lose here

OPP DETECTIVE: I'm sure he does

ARMCHAIR DETECTIVE: With the mattress

ARMCHAIR DETECTIVE: there was a thing that was said to me yesterday that James had Peed on Victoria and that she was going to tell her dad, and that was the specific of it , I am trying to narrow it down as to who told me that.

OPP DETECTIVE: WOW!

ARMCHAIR DETECTIVE: And um there is only one person I talked to yesterday and it was on the pretext of writing my book, and even though Im not writing a book (giggle) but it was a....

OPP DETECTIVE: But that's a GREAT that is a great thing,

ARMCHAIR DETECTIVE: What do you mean

OPP DETECTIVE: But that's a great way a great way of getting people to talk

ARMCHAIR DETECTIVE: Well yeah I know and I can get That's why I can get information from you like I was going to call Kayla Hurst again but I didn't want to get into trouble from you either, you know I want to get People will talk to me that the thing

OPP DETECTIVE: Well Yeah

ARMCHAIR DETECTIVE: and I'll do it free of charge I you know Im not I don't have tunnel vision like the Woodstock police did (giggle) but I'm telling you its weird talking to you like this because you're a police officer, because normally I'm not like this but no its just you know people will talk to me

OPP DETECTIVE: Yeah

ARMCHAIR DETECTIVE: And I can get information that you guys can't.

OPP DETECTIVE: Yep.

ARMCHAIR DETECTIVE: You know what I mean

OPP DETECTIVE: Yep Because you r getting it on a different pretext then we are.

ARMCHAIR DETECTIVE: Exactly and you guys cant lie, and I have nothing to gain or lose from this except for trying to you know

OPP DETECTIVE: Yeah

ARMCHAIR DETECTIVE: This really hit home with me I have an eight year old daughter myself and you know I don't think that this is right this women needs to be put behind bars

OPP DETECTIVE: Yep

ARMCHAIR DETECTIVE: Hopefully sooner than later because what if its not just her own kid what if she goes after someone elses kid

OPP DETECTIVE: Yep

ARMCHAIR DETECTIVE: theres still reports of people being abducted did you notice that

OPP DETECTIVE: yep yeah yep

ARMCHAIR DETECTIVE: What that's similar to the suspect vehicle you know that green vehicle

OPP DETECTIVE: Yep well yeah it's a slippery slope well like I mean that's you know

ARMCHAIR DETECTIVE: So what all do you guys have to have to pick her up

OPP DETECTIVE: I think well to be honest I have no idea what they I know the information that I have and I know the

information but I don't know all the

information the information that they have

ARMCHAIR DETECTIVE: yeah um hmm

OPP DETECTIVE: You know

*ARMCHAIR DETECTIVE: you mean the police
in Woodstock*

*OPP DETECTIVE: Well them and the higher
ups with us*

ARMCHAIR DETECTIVE: Yeah

*OPP DETECTIVE: you know the higher up
investigators*

ARMCHAIR DETECTIVE: um hmm

OPP DETECTIVE: So

ARMCHAIR DETECTIVE: So um

*OPP DETECTIVE: So I just do I just ask
the questions that I'm told I have to*

ARMCHAIR DETECTIVE: do you think there will be an arrest in the imminent future

OPP DETECTIVE: I don't know

ARMCHAIR DETECTIVE: your just trying to get it all together and well I guess you want it all concrete because you've already

OPP DETECTIVE: well yeah

ARMCHAIR DETECTIVE: Has she already served you with legal documents

OPP DETECTIVE: No we haven't heard anything

ARMCHAIR DETECTIVE: Well that's a good thing

OPP DETECTIVE: Yeah we haven't heard anything

ARMCHAIR DETECTIVE: Well that's good

OPP DETECTIVE: So

ARMCHAIR DETECTIVE: Well she probably knows she doesn't want to go up that fuckin alley because shes guilty as sin

OPP DETECTIVE: Yeah Well then there again it is just because we are provincial were bigger

ARMCHAIR DETECTIVE: you're the same as the RCMP

OPP DETECTIVE: We are similar we are provincial

ARMCHAIR DETECTIVE: theyr trying to make a provincial police department here in BC because of that tasering incident and their trying to change that they cant taser in the chest because of that polish fellow cause they translated

OPP DETECTIVE: Oh really yeah I had heard that. So far are you away from Vancouver

ARMCHAIR DETECTIVE: Im about 45   (TAPE

ENDS)

So as the transcript is pretty much self explanatory, lets dissect it just in case you too are sitting there in utter shock. During the course of the conversation at no time does the OPP Detective state that they were convinced they had the correct people in custody. When the Armchair Detective, asks "What do you do in a case like this" the police officer could only provide the answer of "Oh umm I don't know I really don't know." When the armchair detective asks why this happened, the OPP Detective blames it on the pressure of the media, the fact it was a child involved. She never states that she cannot comment on the investigation. When the conversation between the armchair detective and the OPP Detective took place, on October 16, 2009, the case still remained under

investigation although, police had two
suspects in custody. So why was this OPP
Detective disclosing important information
about the case to someone outside the Law
Enforcement Community?

Why would she risk the integrity of the entire
investigation? Perhaps it was because she too had a
heart and felt that an injustice was served, to
Michael Rafertty who was incarcerated for a heinous
crime that perhaps he did not commit and was being
framed.

Could the OPP DETECTIVE be playing the
Armchair detective, trying to make it sound that
she was giving information when actually she
wasn't. After all this detective was a twenty year
veteran of the Ontario Provincial Police
Department.

One can only guess as to why the conversation
took place. Which brings us to the question who is
responsible for the demise of Victoria Stafford?

Did police have who was responsible in custody? Or were the perpetrators still out there?

CHAPTER 5

"Timeline of Events"

Many of the Social Networking sites such as facebook, and Websleuths, had users on their discussion forums that convicted a variety of people being involved in the abduction and murder of Victoria Stafford, in some form or another.

Before the internet most people only heard about cases through, the television, the local newspaper and of course the radio. When the internet was first introduced to Canadians in the 1990's, there was no legal legislation in place with respect to its use. So there was this road to cyberspace, and no rules that surrounded it with the exception, to items that fit in the current laws of the country like Child Pornography. There were no rules or safety nets in place for children, adults or anyone who utilized it in the beginning. This made the internet a playground for criminals.

Take the Victoria Stafford Case, Social Networking Sites such as Facebook & Websleuth forums as an example as users had a heyday. Users were speculating, and providing theory after theory as to who all was involved and as to what exactly happened on that fateful day of April 8, 2009.

What internet users were forgetting when they were basing their assumptions of guilt on others, was that all people are innocent until proven guilty. As well as some of the individuals whom were being accused of having involvement in this heinous case had families of their own and what was being said regardless of any validity to the allegations, was impacting these individuals lives and reputations as well as their emotional well being.

Perhaps we should take a closer examination as to why society jumped all over these individuals in the first place. If we were to see what exactly had happened then maybe a certain level of understanding could come from knowing what exactly occurred and the time frame it happened in.

The Victoria Stafford case was a very complex case from the very beginning, and below is the time line, which was compiled by numerous police press conferences, to newspaper articles, and media reports.

Regardless of the timeline of events, members of society began to base their speculations on the timeline and what certain individuals were doing at specified times.

The timeline provided the fuel for speculations, and theories in the case which ultimately led to negative thoughts about a variety of people. It also led to people accusing individuals falsely of being involved in a crime which there were no charges laid to substantiate the allegations of involvement to the extent that was being alleged.

It is believed that because of the way the timeline occurred that it is the sole reason for many people being accused of the horrific crime, as well as why certain people were being speculated

TIMELINE OF EVENTS

April 8

10:01 a.m. - MR writes on his FaceBook - Everything Good Is Coming My Way

- 12:00 p.m. - TM says that she visited her Grand 'Poppa' at Crescent Care
- 1:38 - TLM's FB activity shows request to exchange phone number - 'disconnected, gimme ur digits - fo rea'
- 3:25 - school dismissed
- 3:32 - Tori seen on video northbound on Fyfe with unidentified female.
- 3:32 or 3:33 - Esso Station Video Showing Rafferty's Car
- 3:45 OR 4:15 - Daryn home (Both times per TM - This shifts the rest of the time line accordingly)

- 4:00/4:15 - 4:30 - TM, LW & DS drive around looking for Tori
- 4:30 TM is dropped off so she can call friends - LW continues to drive around searching
- 5:21 TM calls LW and tells her to go to Police station
- Unknown time - RS calls TM 'will be late picking Tori up'
  . TM replies, "Tori isn't home yet. Hope she isn't missing"
- 6:06 - Missing report filed - The OCPS began its investigation after receiving the initial report
- 6:30 - Rodney is called to inform him that Tori is missing.
- (from 570 news radio interview)
- 7:30 p.m. - Police begin search for Tori
- Early evening - Officer Maitland states MT's car was said to be seen by people at Home Depot Plaza in Guelph with Suspects & Tori in

the Car

- 9:00 - LE Views Video from Esso - Suspect Car there minutes after abduction

April 9

- 12:00 a.m. - Police in other jurisdictions notified
- 3:07 a.m. - LE sent Media notice out
- 11:45 - police helicopter arrives to assist with search
- 4:30 - Southside Pond search by Fire Dept
- Cosmo (TM's dog) eats ???, unknown, possibly plastic or garbage - taken to vet
- LE releases Video from High School of Abductor
- Police say they are looking for a white woman, aged 19-25, about 120-125 pounds, with a black ponytail and who was wearing black jeans and a white puffy jacket.
- Possible sighting in this video of TLM while

Maitland is talking (standing behind her)

- JJ arrives in Woodstock

LE Techs Obtain Surveillance Video from ESSO
station
Between April 8 - 12

- TLM cuts her hair
- Craig Racine, Jessica McDonald and Tina X -
  begin to suspect TLM and have multiple
  conversations with her about Tori's
  disappearance - they contact police during
  this time.
- Police canvas neighborhoods & TLM hides in
  bathroom when LE knocks on Racine's door (same
  link above)

April 10

- Acquaintance of TLM reports to LE that they'd
  given TLM a puffy, white jacket and has
  concerns about the video

- TLM hands out Tori Is Missing flyers
- 4:02 - TLM FB activity - shows another discussion re: exchanging phone numbers 'I'll give u my digz when i get back 2 OTT.'

April 11

- Volunteers accompany police in a second day of searching for Tori.
- Candlelight Vigil for Tori

April 12

- TLM arrested on outstanding warrants/charges. (From Wilson St.). Taken in unmarked car, not in handcuffs.
- 1:50 p.m. - American organization Code Amber News Service issues "Missing Endangered person Alert" for Tori
- 8:00 p.m. - Hundreds gather for a candlelit vigil in the Zellers parking lot

- TM's first 'presser' at vigil

April 13

- Police End Ground Search
- Enhanced Video released

April 14

- Police Defend Not Issuing Amber Alert

April 15

- TM Expresses that Tori's Disappearance Should be Treated as Abduction
- TM states she 'has not done drugs since high school'
- News comes out about James Goris 3rd Appearance in Court regarding Theft under $5,000 charge

April 16

- Woodstock Rally & Balloon Release

- TM urges Police to Treat Case as Abduction. 30

  LE around the clock. 500 Tips so far

April 17

- OPP Take Lead in Case Investigation

April 19

- LE Reports >1,000 Tips To Date
- Symbolic Walk on College St. Dozens of people

April 21

- Composite Sketch Released
- Lie Detector Tests disclosed to media

April 22

- Cambridge Woman Mistakenly Arrest then

  Released

April 23

- Mysterious Benefactor Limo Ride

April 24

- Daryn's 11th Birthday

April 25

- Stafford case featured on Americas Most Wanted television show.

April 27

- TM Releases News of Mysterious Benefactor & Limo Ride Publicly

April 28

- Oxford Police Announce $50,000 Reward

MAY 1

- <u>Police Ask Farmers to Be Vigilant</u>

May 2

- <u>'Tori's Ride Home' Motorcycle ride May 2nd.</u>

May 4

- <u>LE Release VOI Images</u>

- <u>JJ TM's brother returns to Alberta. (per TM press conf)</u>

May 5

- <u>RS Makes Another Plea for Tori's Release</u>

- <u>TM Absent from Press Conference for the 1st Time</u>

- <u>Police Search Door-to-door Again in Woodstock</u>

May 6

- <u>TM believes daughter still alive</u>

- <u>Police search homes in Cluny, Alberta.</u>
- <u>TM Confirms LE Seized Her Computer Earlier in Case</u>

<u>May 7</u>

- <u>Daryn Joins TM & RS at Press Conference</u>
- <u>Courtice Balloon Launch</u>
- <u>SL Reacts - 'It's Not Me</u>

<u>May 8</u>

- <u>TM Reports Computers Seized & JJ's & his Mom's Homes recently searched in AB</u>
- <u>Sarah L reacts "It's not me"</u>

<u>May 10 (Mother'sDay)</u>

<u>May 12</u>

- <u>Cosmo (TM's dog) is picked up from the Vet</u>

<u>May 13</u>

- Tara reads Tori Love Letter (debate - written on Mom's Day?)

May 14

- TM Admits Drug Problem

May 15th

- Racine & JMcD see MR in the area
- RS & TM Bicker During PC
- Racine & JMcd email LE license plate of MTR to police

- 100 Officers Working the Case

May 17

- Candlelight Vigil Victoria Park, London

May 18 (Victoria Day)

- Float Honoring Tori In Woodstock Victoria Day

Parade

- **Vigil in Ingersoll at Memorial Park**

May 19

- RS & TM announce they have accepted help from PI
- Approx 10:30 - 11:00 p.m. - MR arrested

May 20 (Day 1 of Remains Search) DAY 42

- ARRESTS - OPP Major Development Release
- Video of Announcement

- Charged are: 18-year-old **Terri-Lynn McClintic** is charged with the following Criminal Code Charges:
  - Accessory After The Fact To Murder
  - Abduction Of A Person Under Sixteen

- 28-year-old **Michael Rafferty** is charged with the following Criminal Code Charges:
  - First Degree Murder
  - Abduction Of A Person Under Sixteen

- TLM & MR Both Appear in Court - (Oxford County Court House) - Remanded into Custody until May 28t
- 4:00 p.m. Police Search Rockwood Area (wellington

22 & #6)

- Evening - Chopper Search Moves 10 Miles N - tow Fergus

- Rob S Lunges for MR and shouts Expletives as MR Leaves Court

- Students at Tori's School are Informed She is D

- Police Confirm TM Knows TLM

- RS - "I Can't Believe She's Dead"

-

  'Tori Is Missing' picture remains on MR's House">'Tori Is Missing' picture remains on MR' House

- Missing Alert for Tori Canceled

- Photo Gallery of Arrests (LFP Keeps Adding Phot Check Often)

- TLM Begins Assisting Police With Search

- TLM is Held Daily at the Oxford Community Polic Station until May 23rd

May 21 (Day 2 of Remains Search)

- Forensics Van at TM's for DNA Profile (tooth, shoes)
- Tara Lashes out at LE
- OPP Search Guelph Car Washes
- Tara denies buying drugs from TLM
- TLM helps with Search For Tori's Body
- LE Cordons Off Garbage Dumpster Near Fergus
- Const. Glen Childerley says the search for Tori's body will be a long and complex process.
- Counselors at Tori's School
- Last Tea Party For Tori - Thrown by her Friends
- Police Release Photos of 2003 Honda
- Police Seize MR's Honda (sometime between 20th - 21st)

May 22 (Day 3 of Remains Search)

- Police release Photos of Suspect MR's Vehicle (believed to have been in vicinity of Guelph Home Depot April 8th)
- Carol M., TLM's adoptive Mother, says TLM met Tori

through the dogs. Tori talked to TLM about one Carol's dogs, Precious

- Carol states she met TM & JG previously when th wanted to breed their dog.
- TM Doesn't Think TLM Will be of any 'Help'
- TM:"Just remember her because she was the prettiest, most beautiful little girl in the world."
- Former Addicts/Dealers Discuss OXY Trade & Use Woodstock

May 23 (Day 4 of Remains Search)

- MR's Ex-GF Describes their Former Relationship
- LW Talks About Puppy for Tori & Forgiveness
- Police Tactics Questioned
- PM Harper says "Tori is in a Better Place"
- Ontario Provincial Police Commissioner Julian Fantino (Top Cop) Draws Parallel Between Tori's Case & Bernardo's Victims
- Tara Thanks Community

May 24 (Day 5 of Remains Search)

- 10:00 p.m. - Court Order Allowing McClintic to Assist With Search Expires
- Tori Stafford investigators hunt for missing car seat
- McClintic In Elgin-Middlesex Detention Centre
- Tara's Family Disputes Drug Connection
- Police Ask Woodstock Businesses for More Surveillance Video

May 25 (Day 6 of Remains Search)

(National Missing Children's Day)

- LE Inspect Car Seat Found in Kitchener - Sent to Tillsonburg for OPP Forensic Testing
- McClintic no longer assisting with the search.
- LE Search Bellwood & Guelph Lakes with Sonar
- RS States That He Feels Tori Was Targeted For Abduction
- Tori's accused killer on suicide watch in Elgin-

Middlesex Detention Center

May 26

- Report: <u>LE Views Video from Esso on April 8th</u> <u>Suspect Car there minutes after abduction</u>
- <u>MR Exercising His Right to Remain Silent</u>

May 28

- Suspects remanded in custody.

May 29

- Police release to the public that the remains Victoria Stafford may never be found.

May 30

- RS & TM Plan to hold public memorial for Victo on June 6th 2009 at the Calvary Pentecostal Chu at 1:00 pm in Woodstock, although her body had been found as of yet.

June 2

- TLM Spends her 19th birthday incarcerated at the London Detention Center.

June 6

- Tori's Memorial Service

July 19

- Victoria Staffords remains are found in Mt. Forest by a veteran detective who had been working the case.

CHAPTER 6

"The Speculations & Theories"

The case created quite the stir of speculations and theories through the community of Woodstock. Some people were getting absolutely tired of listening to all the hubbub of the case, and others were sitting on pins and needles just waiting with bated breath to see if there would be any new arrests in the Imminent Future. Specifically, people wanted to know the one leading question did Tara McDonald & James Goris, have anything to do with Victoria's abduction and demise.

Other questions the public thirsted for answers for were if there was a drug debt, whether or not there was gang involvement, and whether or not there was a cult involved. It seemed that as days continued to go by, the public was no closer to getting their answers then the media.

So in the meantime while the world awaited the trial of 19 year old Terri-Lynn Mcclintic, and Michael Thomas Rafferty, the spectators were forced to rely on the chat forums of facebook and other websites such as Websleuths.

People began to speculate and theorize what they felt happened on that frightful day in April.

Facebook forum discussion groups started popping up groups called "Victoria Stafford Opinion, Case, and Analysis", "Say whatever you $$>#@ Want to Say", Michael Rafferty & Terri-Lynn Mcclintic are Innocent, Profiting from Crime in Canada is Wrong, Non Bashing Group, and many more. When one group would get shut down for infringement of Facebooks terms of use, another one the same would pop up to take its place. It was in these groups where speculations flew, pictures and documents where publication bans prevented such documents being published were posted for the world to see. Controlling as to what was being posted in these forums was absolutely impossible, although Facebook received thousands of complaints about specified content, and take it down the information would be reposed by another group or party. So to keep the lid on it was absolutely, a task on its own.

Contacting police agencies regarding harassment on facebook and other sites proved to become fruitless as well as Law Enforcement Agencies were not equipped to handle internet crime that was not clearly defined as a crime like fraud or pornographic pictures of children. Victims of the harassment were just told "STAY OF THE INTERNET", meanwhile users were posting the physical addresses and phone numbers, of individuals whom they didn't agree with what the person was posting. In some instances people were posting pictures of other members children for the world to see. It became a downright nasty situation, and no one seemed to be able to do anything about it.

There was very little anyone could do if they were the brunt of people's harassments, or speculations. Even lawyers wouldn't touch it as again it was too difficult to prosecute.

Below is the complete transcript of one of the most controversial secret Social Medium Groups that discussed the Victoria Stafford Case. It was the group that started the speculations about who was responsible.

Topic: **Tara will have a hard time suing, if this case got thrown out!!**

Displaying all 5 posts by 4 people.

Barb Returns (Kitchener, ON) wrote on July 2, 2009 at 10:33pm

True...what a terrible story...

But in Tara's case...she can't do a damn thing... what's she gonna sue us for? For repeating everything that came straight out from her own mouth? I honestly for the life of me can't imagine what the law suit would say... this is a public forum no different than if we were all sitting in a cafe somewhere talking about the case in the news. Should she call the police and have an attorney file law suits on everyone in a cafe that talks about the case that's in the newspaper, on tv, on internet and chatted about in social settings? It's all ludicrous. She's just pissed off that she can't manipulate and control things and she's lashing out

Post #3

Joanna Ferri replied to Barb's poston July 2, 2009 at 10:40pm

Completely agree with you...If anything she is totally acting like the 'bully' in this situation, her way or no way. . jmo

Post #4

1 reply

Misty Wells wrote on July 3, 2009 at 6:36pm

for sueing me for merging pictures together? I gave an open apology to Tara, but I got dissed from all her friends, but thats alright because I know I was wrong in doing that. There are alot of people who merged pictures together? its funny Tara has never said anything way before until the end?

Post #6

Misty Wells wrote on July 3, 2009 at 8:29pm

I shoudnt feel bad you're right I have always been fair in what I say I have seen alot worse been said on here. Its a bunch of BS.

Topic: <u>**Look out she is Recrouting her spies....LMAO**</u>

<u>Delete Topic</u>|<u>Reply to Topic</u>

Displaying all 5 posts by 5 people.

Post #1

1 reply

Denise Martin (Toronto, ON) wrote on June 27, 2009
at 6:30pm

Tara McDonald (London, ON) wrote
at 11:55am
My request is...if anyone sees anyone saying
anything that is inappropriate, you be the judge,
just copy and paste it in my inbox and I'll print
it out. I've had it up to here -------> with all
the BS. So the more eyes out there, the better,
they have their creepers, and I'll have mine

Tara McDonald (London, ON) wrote
at 12:11pm
There will be repercussions for the people who have
been extremely hurtful, and continuously posting
incorrect info....
Report
found this on another group and wanted to share
this....like seriously come on .....LOL

Post #2

<u>Rosie Smart</u> replied to <u>Denise's post</u>on June 27, 2009 at 6:45pm

LOL saw that already. She is trying to make a case but it wont work.

Post deleted on June 27, 2009 at 7:00pm

Post #4

<u>Judy Manzo</u> (Kitchener, ON) wrote on June 27, 2009 at 9:13pm

My goodness her hit list is going to be mighty large, I guess she figures that her welfare cheque is going to be enough to hire people to take care of TLM and the rest of us who think there is more to this story....

Post #5

Heather Gogan (Halifax, NS) wrote on July 4, 2009 at 5:42pm

she is going to sue everyone for slander and make a bundle...lol

Topic: Daryn's Bestfriend?

Delete Topic|Reply to Topic

Displaying all 21 posts by 9 people.

Post #1

Rosie Smart wrote on June 27, 2009 at 10:54am

Tara McDonald I love you baby...and I'm so glad I have you in my life. Your Daryn's best friend, as well as mine, and I cannot wait to be your wifey. You are so strong and I feel so safe with you as my partner. If it wasn't for you, over the last 3 months, I don't know what Daryn and I would of done without you. You are my best friend, my lover, my strength, you are my everything. October can't come fast enough...and neither can November *WINK WINK*

I love you babe!!!!

Tara wrote this on James FB wall. Also wonder why JG just added ?Accepted Tara as a friend?

Post #2

Barb Returns (Kitchener, ON) wrote on June 27, 2009 at 2:29pm

Yechhhhhh... anyone know where the ant-acids are?

If she's already pregnant, no ant-acids will help... I'll be puking my guts. It's not bad enough she's put two children in excessive danger with her behaviors and neglect and one of them DIES but now she wants to being more children in to this f'ing nightmare? Bloody-hell!

Post #3

1 reply

Debbie Weir Cairns (London, ON) wrote on June 28, 2009 at 6:11am

The only reason for her to post this for the whole world to see is to taunt people. Otherwise, she could just tell him in person right? I think she is playing head games!

Post #4

Rosie Smart replied to Debbie's post on June 28, 2009 at 6:32am

For sure!

Post #5

Dawn Bossert MacEachern wrote on June 28, 2009 at 9:25am yes, head games and to see how far news will travel...otherwise you dont post stuff like that for all to see....

Post #6

1 reply

Misty Wells wrote on June 28, 2009 at 10:52am

Daryn and James went to Wrestling theres "hot girls hot boys" there

Post deleted on June 28, 2009 at 10:59am

Post #8

Misty Wells wrote on June 28, 2009 at 11:10am

Tara McDonald (London, ON) wrote

at 11:43am

I think these are local wrestlers...but there's a really hot girl wrestler that both of my boys are excited to see

i was just referring to that James and Daryn went to wrestling that was James father's day gift.

everytime i think of James being a father to Daryn it makes me sick after finding out about those allegations

Post #9

1 reply

Frances Clarke wrote on June 28, 2009 at 11:14am

I don't understand how she can still function??...never mind be excited about anything, I am sorry but I would not be able to do anything if one of my Children went missing and then was murdered, is this normal behavior?

Someone needs to call a news show she is acting like Caysie Anthony!!

Post #10

<u>Sandie Wales Kay</u> (Toronto, ON) replied to <u>Frances's post</u> on June 28, 2009 at 11:23am

How observant Frances.... hell yah!

Post #11

1 reply

Dawn Bossert MacEachern wrote on June 28, 2009 at 11:28am

taking a preadolescent boy to see "hot girl wrestlers"????????
& where did the money for the tickets come from????

Post #12

1 reply

Dawn Bossert MacEachern wrote on June 28, 2009 at 11:29am

& was Daryn with Rodney at all for Father's Day?????

Post #13

1 reply

Sandie Wales Kay (Toronto, ON) replied to Dawn's post on June 28, 2009 at 11:30am

You and me and other tax payers.... did you not get your thank you note.

Post #15

Dawn Bossert MacEachern replied to Sandy's post on June 28, 2009 at 11:51am

Sandie...THEY MISPLACED MY TY NOTE!!!!!!

Post #16

1 reply

Dawn Bossert MacEachern replied to Rosie's post on June 28, 2009 at 11:56am

I think Barb saw Rodney and Daryn bike riding together around that time but not sure what day, so possibly Daryn spent a day with Daddy and a day with James...

Post #17

Misty Wells wrote on June 28, 2009 at 12:32pm

VIP TICKETS she said

Post #18

1 reply

Barb Returns (Kitchener, ON) replied to Dawn's post on June 28, 2009 at 1:23pm

No it was this past Tuesday Dawn...I took my daughter to her piano exam and had to kill time until she finished so I drove around the corner to Tara's place. That's when Daryn and Rodney pulled up on their bikes.

But glad to know my hard earned tax dollars are

spent on drugs, drinking, fake high fashion garbage and Wrestling tickets, rather than food, clothing and shelter for 2 (now only 1 for the time being) child(ren). :o/

Post #19

Dawn Bossert MacEachern replied to Barb's post on June 28, 2009 at 1:29pm

Don't forget "tea parties" Barb!!!!! For a whole group of people....

Post #20

Barb Returns (Kitchener, ON) wrote on June 28, 2009 at 2:11pm

LOL..oh right Dawn...the "tea" parties. ;o)

Post #21

Heather Gogan (Halifax, NS) wrote on July 4, 2009 at 5:55pm

wow, what a person she is....unreal

Topic: This has done it for me. I am Sick Now!

Delete Topic|Reply to Topic

Displaying all 15 posts by 9 people.

Post #1

1 reply

Rosie Smart wrote on June 27, 2009 at 8:57pm

Tara McDonald My cell has no time on it...I got your text to landline, those things crack me up!!! I'm going to be in London for the night, staying at my best friends place for a little get a way. I found some pretty funny Polaroid photos of us from the old' H.P. LOL The word Polaroid should say it all...WE ARE OLD!!!! We ran into an old friend of ours a few weeks ago...ask me when we're talking one on one and I'll fill you in...

She really is acting like Tori was never a part of her life! Like she was never missing or born or something! Makes me Sick!!!

Post #2

Judy Manzo (Kitchener, ON) wrote on June 27, 2009 at 9:09pm

OMG...she has no time on her cell...guess she should maybe do another fund raiser to help her out with that.

Post deleted on June 27, 2009 at 10:18pm

Post #4

1 reply

Diane Ross (St. Catharine's / Niagara, ON) wrote on June 27, 2009 at 10:51pm

Where are you finding these posts, Rosie?

Post #5

1 reply

Rosie Smart replied to Diane's post on June 28,
2009 at 7:15am

I have spies all over Tara FB lol

Post #6

Rosie Smart wrote on June 28, 2009 at 7:15am

Polaroid photos of us from the old' H.P. LOL
What is H.P.?

Post #7

1 reply

Diane Ross (St. Catharine's / Niagara, ON) replied
to Rosie's post on June 28, 2009 at 8:34am

lol, you sneak!! ;-)

HP is Huron Park Secondary School--where she went to high school

Post deleted on June 28, 2009 at 8:34am

Post #9

1 reply

Barb Returns (Kitchener, ON) replied to post on June 28, 2009 at 2:54pm

Rosie...you are SOOOOO right... it's like Tori never existed... it's not normal no matter what reason you give for her current behavior. It's only been 5 weeks since she's known Tori to be deceased. I still can't even sit down to read a book...took all my library books back to the library b/c I can't concentrate since Tori went missing. But Tara can party, go on trips, plan tubal reversals and wedding, play on chat groups, plan "tea" parties, write love letters to James and make multiple threats to sue people on various websites. Where does this woman find the TIME let alone the emotional fortitude to move COMPLETELY on 5 weeks after being told her beloved daughter is dead and not just dead but a car accident or unknown heart defect...but from a BRUTAL ABDUCTION AND MURDER?!

PLEASE! She's an "abomination".

Post #10

Judy Manzo (Kitchener, ON) replied to post on June 29, 2009 at 11:47am

Barb I don't get this either...I have nothing to compare in my life with the abduction and murder of a child. However, I can say ... if anything were to happen to my children or grand child...I do not know how I would act, or how I would feel. But ... one thing is for sure, I know that in the first 5 weeks, I wouldn't be planning have the social events that Ms. TM has been planning.

I understand and get it that life does continue moving regardless...but .. I strongly feel that TM needs to do further reading and research on the stages of grieving ...

I'm not sure who her counselor is that she is seeing, but, damn they are good if they can get her thru years and years of what she should be feeling, all over with in this short time.

Post #11

2 replies

Colette Orr wrote on June 29, 2009 at 1:26pm

I lost my hubby of 27 years...in a tragic motor vehicle accident 10 years ago....all I got were the remains of his body. I could not get any closure b/c there was no body. There were no good-byes.

I realize this is nothing compared to losing a child, but in the same sense I have gone thru the 7 steps of grief...not once, not twice but over & over again; as well as much Bereavement Counseling. There is no way in hell Tara has done any grieving...not even started to grieve. It's like this never even happened to her. I was unable to cope w/anything for over a year & was trying to raise 2 young children @ that time.

Life does go on, but for Tara, live has not even stopped yet. She's a dam disgrace to the human race, let alone to Mom's. She literally disgusts me......and makes me so dam angry with her stupid talk and actions....grrrr

Post #12

Sandie Wales Kay (Toronto, ON) replied to post on June 29, 2009 at 1:42pm

"She literally disgusts me......and makes me so dam angry with her stupid talk and actions....grrrr"

You and all us "normal" folk Colette. Well said.

Post #13

1 reply

Sandie Wales Kay (Toronto, ON) replied to post on June 29, 2009 at 1:44pm

It's as if she actually has knowledge that she is not dead and sees no need to grieve. Then, she laughs at us because we are the fools being sucked in.

Post #14

Colette Orr replied to post on June 29, 2009 at 2:44pm

Yessssss & I don't believe she is "in denial" either b/c again, if she were in denial she would not be acting the way she does. I've said it before & I will say it yet again...TARA is all about TARA.....It just doesn't seem to matter to her that her child has gone missing & presumed dead. I suppose those oxy's must do wonders for you! (lol).....& as she herself stated "they make everything seem ok"......blahhhh Tara,,,One day Karma is gonna come your way & I hope when it does it bites you so hard in the ass....

Post #15

Heather Gogan (Halifax, NS) wrote on July 4, 2009 at 6:01pm

I am sure it will Colette, so sure....Tara is ridiculous...I think I would have been committed to the hospital or something cause I really don't think I could survive losing my child...

Topic: **Rodney Stafford has worn through two pairs of running shoes**

Delete Topic|Reply to Topic

Displaying all 13 posts by 8 people.

Post #1

1 reply

Rosie Smart wrote on June 27, 2009 at 4:30pm

Rod has searched and search and I am sure still searching for Tori as Tara has never SEARCHED is making Tea Party arrangements.

She makes herself look guilty of knowing something about Tori disappearance!

Post #2

Judy Manzo (Kitchener, ON) wrote on June 27, 2009 at 5:16pm

I agree with you Rosie...Poor Rodney ... it's amazing how Tara did not show any emotion regarding her daughter (to the public) about her daughter prior to the arrests...and since then it seems that making new friends who can help scrapbook, plan a wedding, and now have "tea parties" seems to be more important then her daughter...very disgusting.

Post #3

Colette Orr wrote on June 27, 2009 at 5:39pm

Rodney needs closure; whereas to Tara, it seems she already has closure...I find this very strange ,.....even to the point where she is talking about having another child.....<cringes> @ the thought of her parenting another child....

Post deleted on June 27, 2009 at 10:27pm

Post #5

Debbie Weir Cairns (London, ON) replied to Mel's poston June 28, 2009 at 2:09am

They will if you pay to have it done. I heard it costs $3000-5000 to have the operation.

Post #6

1 reply

<u>Debbie Weir Cairns</u> (London, ON) replied to <u>Rosie's post</u>on June 28, 2009 at 2:10am

That is so sad about Rodney, I feel so bad for him. It must break his heart even more knowing what TM is doing and planning. Poor guy!

Post #7

1 reply

<u>Rosie Smart</u> replied to <u>Debbie's post</u>on June 28, 2009 at 6:37am

Other mothers of mising kids are still LOOKING for there kids and doing what ever it takes. BUt not Tara????

Post #8

1 reply

Colette Orr replied to <u>Rosie's post</u>on June 28, 2009 at 7:38am

Rosie.....Why would Tara be looking for Tori NOW; she's NEVER looked before....She's much 2 busy doing her nails, planning her wedding & having JG literally hanging off of her .....and don't 4get "TARA IS ALL ABOUT TARA".......blahhhhhh

Post #9

<u>Rosie Smart</u> replied to <u>Colette's post</u>on June 28, 2009 at 7:41am

Tara was finally gonna post some posters as she said in Last pc that Tuesday. That there were no posters at Niagra border. And she was going to do that that weekend. Hmmmmm Finally she was going to do something to help and the two were arressted. Wonder if she new TLM was gonna confess.

However i think TLM is gonna renag. As She never confessed to Murder.

Post #10

Rosie Smart wrote on June 28, 2009 at 7:41am

Wonder what Rod is doing these days?

Post #11

1 reply

Charlotte Beal wrote on June 28, 2009 at 4:18pm

Wasnt it said TLM was recanting?

Post #12

Dawn Bossert MacEachern replied to Charlotte's poston June 28, 2009 at 8:06pm

havent heard that, but it wouldnt surprise me if she does

Post #13

Heather Gogan (Halifax, NS) wrote on July 4, 2009 at 6:28pm

I heard that she was recanting...can't remember where I read it though....

The John Deer Building

Back to Victoria Stafford Group For Those Who Believe There Is More To This CASE!!

Topic: The John Deer Building

Delete Topic|Reply to Topic

Displaying all 13 posts by 7 people.

Post #1

Rosie Smart wrote on June 28, 2009 at 7:38am

80 to 100 cops still on Tori case

http://cnews.canoe.ca/CNEWS/Canada/2009/06/24/99093

41-sun.html

Last I heard police are still using this building.
Some say the lot was full others said 12-15 cars??

Post #2

Diane Ross (St. Catharines / Niagara, ON) wrote on
June 28, 2009 at 8:35am

depends on when you drive by, some days there are
more cars there than others.

Post #3

1 reply

Rosie Smart wrote on June 29, 2009 at 8:20pm

On another forum, It was said that there was police from all over Ontario

Wow now that sean, Roxxy bf is posting about Roxxy makes me think that this is why.JMO

Post #4

1 reply

Dawn Bossert MacEachern replied to Rosie's poston June 29, 2009 at 8:24pm

when were there police from all over????? today or what???
that is certainly interesting...this situation has so many threads to it...i can see there being investigators from all around...thats a good thing!!!! lets get this dealt with...

Post #5

1 reply

Rosie Smart replied to Dawn's poston June 29, 2009
at 8:26pm

It was last week. I forget where I read that BUT
now to come to think of it. It was posted on my old
group I think. will look around or if anyone
remembers please mention it. Thanks

Post #6

1 reply

Judy Manzo (Kitchener, ON) replied to Rosie's
poston June 29, 2009 at 8:36pm

Rosie that WAS posted on the old group....is it any
wonder that cops are involved from all over Ontario
... and now, Edmonton....

Post #7

Rosie Smart replied to Judy's poston June 29, 2009
at 8:37pm

Thanks Judy I knew I read that lol

Post #8

2 replies

Rosie Smart wrote on July 1, 2009 at 12:11pm

Heather Ann Daley-Hall (London, ON) wrote15 minutes ago
Drove by this morning parking lot was full of cars...just drove by and the parking lot is full....night before they made the arrests the parking lot was the same...got a gut feeling something is going down......hopefully we hear something tomorrow or later tonight

Update was posted on another group. Thought it was needed here as well.

Post #9

Dawn Bossert MacEachern wrote on July 1, 2009 at 1:11pm

interesting its full on Canada Day!!!!!

were there out of province licence plates, did u notice????

certainly hope something is coming down...we all need closure soon

Post #10

You replied to Rosie's post on July 1, 2009 at 2:35pm

Is there a possibility that people use that parking lot other than the POLICE? Also, its Canada Day, it is possible they are going over all the evidence they have, is it usual to have this many people in the John deer Building?

Delete Post

Post #11

Judy Manzo (Kitchener, ON) replied to Rosie's post on July 1, 2009 at 5:04pm thanks for that update Rosie ... even if it was from another board.

This must be some investigation taking place...I have read that police in Edmonton are involved as well .. so who knows which other detachments in other provinces are involved too.

I hope this writer is correct that we are going to hear something soon...

Post #12

Janet Hall wrote on July 3, 2009 at 10:08am

Just curious what the parking lot is like these days, it was interesting that there was so many vehicles at the building on the 1st, is it still as busy ? I sure hope so.

Post #13

Heather Gogan (Halifax, NS) wrote on July 4, 2009 at 6:56pm

was wondering about an update are there still alot of cars at the building??

Topic: <u>IMO ... do you think TM will request a package from the Criminal Compensation Board?</u>

<u>Delete Topic</u>|<u>Reply to Topic</u>

Displaying posts 1 - 30 out of 57 by 14 people.

Post #1

1 reply

<u>Rosie Smart</u> wrote on June 29, 2009 at 7:22pm

Makes me think she might just do that as everything is money money money with her.

She needs to pay for a wedding tubes untied and possibly retied? Where's the money coming from?

http://www.courtprep.ca/en/witnessTips/cic.asp

What do you think?

Post #2

Dawn Bossert MacEachern wrote on June 29, 2009 at 7:31pm

highly possible i would imagine, but she has to be for sure off the suspect llist first id think, and i dont think they have done that yet...

Post #3

Judy Manzo (Kitchener, ON) wrote on June 29, 2009 at 7:34pm

Well why wouldnt she attempt to get money from here...TM has tried every angle possible...she's collecting welfare (she's capable of working)...she tried to get people to help pay her phone bill when all of this start (get a job)...she's got her name on the trust fund (not sure who would donate to that)... so why not the criminal compensation board....

BUT...she wont get funds anytime soon..

Post #5

3 replies

Rosie Smart replied to Lisa's poston June 29, 2009 at 7:45pm

The Criminal Injuries Compensation Board helps people who have been injured directly whether physically, psychologically or both and people harmed as a result of injury to another, such as the children of a murder victim.

Rosie Smart replied to Rosie's poston June 29, 2009 at 7:45pm

$$$$$$$$$

Post #7

Lisa Klein-Gunnewiek (Kingston, ON) replied to Rosie's poston June 29, 2009 at 7:46pm

Thanks!

Post #8

2 replies

Judy Manzo (Kitchener, ON) replied to Rosie's poston June 29, 2009 at 7:48pm

Rosie a few years back I had to apply for this (for my son street fight)....
It took almost two years for funds to come thru, I had to have all doctors fill out their portion of the forms stating in extent to his injuries ... and it took almost two years for funds...
I realize that pain and suffering is what makes up the most for settlements but the criminal compensation board does have a ceiling to what they pay out.

Post #9

Rosie Smart replied to Judy's poston June 29, 2009 at 8:06pm

Glad to hear it will take a while.

Post #10

1 reply

Dawn Bossert MacEachern wrote on June 29, 2009 at 8:10pm

yes, im glad it will take awhile too...then the case will be better understood and all the players too, hopefully...

I can see Daryn getting compensation for it...i would agree with that for the trauma he is going thru...

Post #11

2 replies

Rosie Smart replied to Dawn's poston June 29, 2009 at 8:18pm

Yes. I understand that. BUt I have seen Tara time and time again go for money . Like it is her objective.

Why is Tara on fb so much where is Daryn? He needs his mom to be with him doing whatever not watching her sit on the damn computer!

Post #12

1 reply

Dawn Bossert MacEachern replied to Rosie's poston June 29, 2009 at 8:22pm

I certainly agree that he needs his mom to be a mom...not sure where he is...Barb saw him riding his bike with his Dad awhile back and Tara has spoken of him going places with JG, but other than that, im not certain...

i hope he gets to spend time with his grandma's & his Dads family this summer...he needs to get away from Frances street and have fun...take his mind off things and let him be a kid...

Post #13

Judy Manzo (Kitchener, ON) replied to Dawn's post on June 29, 2009 at 8:39pm

I'm so glad to hear that Daryn has been seen with his Dad...I think if anyone is going to be able to help that little boy thru all of this it's going to be his dad, and his dad's family.
They seem to be the ones with the family values

Post deleted on June 29, 2009 at 10:08pm

Post #15

1 reply

Barb Returns (Kitchener, ON) wrote on June 29, 2009 at 11:07pm

Tara better be careful...if she has anything at all to do with Tori being abducted and she accepts money for anything related to Tori's death, she could find herself in a heap more trouble down the road.

Post deleted on June 30, 2009 at 6:39am

Post #17

Gaylene Bowman wrote on June 30, 2009 at 8:18am

Well well well isnt that interesting, of course she will be entitled under the Ontario Law if she is in fact eligable but as Barb has said...that can open doors to even further charges if she is even remotely related to anything that has gone down...time will tell all...and sooner or later ALL people involved in Tori's dissapearance will pay for their sick ways. It does take a year for any decision for compensation..so by then hopefully those involved will all be arraigned. Too bad this trial wouldnt be concluded faster so we could all see the outcome sooner.

Post #18

Judy Manzo (Kitchener, ON) replied to Rosie's poston June 30, 2009 at 8:33am

Does it really surprise you that one of her "followers" doesnt believe in her.
I cant believe that those who are "claiming" to be in support of her dont see her tacky was, and her lies.

I understand that there would be a time frame of when you would be able to apply to the criminal compensation board, but, one would think that at this point a parent would still be hanging onto the hope that their child is still alive and would be waiting longer to make such an application.
She is just disgusting.

Post #19

1 reply

Barb Returns (Kitchener, ON) replied to Rosie's poston June 30, 2009 at 8:50am

""Why is Tara on fb so much where is Daryn? He needs his mom to be with him doing whatever not watching her sit on the damn computer!""

Oy Rosie...you don't expect her to get up off her arse for her SON when her own daughter was missing due to abduction and she IN HER OWN WORDS said she had "done NOTHING to find her"... tsk tsk...you over-estimate Tara ;o) (teasing Rosie...just teasing)

Post deleted on June 30, 2009 at 8:54am

Post #21

1 reply

Barb Returns (Kitchener, ON) replied to Rosie's post on June 30, 2009 at 9:02am

I'm sure she and James had already researched it.

Post deleted on June 30, 2009 at 9:03am

Post #23

Barb Returns (Kitchener, ON) wrote on June 30, 2009 at 9:08am

Yes and lets hope if they DID research it that it was found in the history of the hard drive. Or that 'something' was found of importance.

Post #24

1 reply

Rosie Smart wrote on June 30, 2009 at 1:16pm

We have a mole! This thread about compansation fund is being talked about on Rose group.

Post #25

Judy Manzo (Kitchener, ON) wrote on June 30, 2009 at 1:18pm

OMG....are you going to be able to figure out who it is Rosie....

Post #26

Misty Wells wrote on June 30, 2009 at 1:27pm

I seen that Rosie and the thing is the person that started it isnt even in your group Rosie

Post #27

1 reply

Dawn Bossert MacEachern replied to Rosie's post on June 30, 2009 at 1:39pm

so someone is reporting to someone else and they are posting then....

Post #28

Rosie Smart replied to Dawn's post on June 30, 2009 at 1:40pm

Dont know. Just two people were talking about it on rose group and niether are in this group.

Post #29

Dawn Bossert MacEachern wrote on June 30, 2009 at 1:51pm

interesting....

Post #30

Joanna Ferri wrote on June 30, 2009 at 2:15pm

I'm a member of that group as well Rosie..I do most of my lurking in there...for the most part I believe the ones who are constantly chatting it up in there are TM supporters...

Tiffany Alleo suggested something about JG might benefit (money)from TM by marrying her..

I do not believe ever seeing this person post anywhere.

Does anyone know her?

Back to Victoria Stafford Group For Those Who Believe There Is More To This CASE!!

Topic: IMO ... do you think TM will request a package from the Criminal Compensation Board?

Displaying posts 31 - 57 out of 57 by 14 people.

Judy Manzo (Kitchener, ON) wrote on June 30, 2009 at 2:19pm

Interesting Joanna...that's really interesting...

Becky Roach wrote on June 30, 2009 at 4:45pm

tm admitted to filing for it?? seriously messed up wow! i had no idea until reading this thread there was such a thing...does not surprise me one bit that tara knew about this and on top of that is filing for it when her baby girls body hasn't even been found yet.

AND planning for things in the near future that will require money. my god

Post #33

1 reply

Rosie Smart replied to Becky's post on June 30, 2009 at 4:48pm

She told a friend that I know lol She never told me directly. Tara really needs to know who her friends are lol

Post #34

Dawn Bossert MacEachern wrote on June 30, 2009 at 4:56pm

Tara appears to be her own worst enemy.....she needs to learn discretion...doesnt have any idea how to be discreet with her talk or actions...sad actually, very sad...

Post #35

Judy Manzo (Kitchener, ON) replied to Rosie's post on June 30, 2009 at 7:16pm

Tara seems to think that she is the only one who can do a cover up....looks good on her...wonder what else she will run her mouth off about to her so called friends.

Post deleted on June 30, 2009 at 10:53pm

Post #37

Gaylene Bowman wrote on July 1, 2009 at 5:27am

I dont think they would even look at a payout until the case has been heard, the evidence re: the crime made available to the board(which wont happen until after the case has been heard) and they have proof certain that Tori has passed on. It would make no sense for them to award any money for a victim of a crime when there are no parties even tried and found guilty of anything yet. I dont think it will happen until after the trial and verdict, if then.

Post #38

1 reply

Debbie Weir Cairns (London, ON) wrote on July 1, 2009 at 6:04am

If it is true that she has applied for this compensation, I find this very interesting. When did she find out about this being available? Before Tori went missing or after?

It strikes me as a bit premature not to mention cold hearted, considering a body has not even been found yet.

I would be very interested to see if the police find any information about this in the history of her computer during the weeks before or shortly after Tori disappearance.

I had never heard of this in my life and wouldn't even think to check something like this out if I had lost a child. Especially, considering how recent the whole case is. I could understand a year later or something, but this soon after?

She is one piece of work isn't she?

Post #39

Rosie Smart replied to Debbie's post on July 1, 2009 at 6:15am

I could see if She was working at the time Tori went missing. And needed help with bills etc. But welfare is paying her way. No need to jump on this when Tori hasnt even been found yet.

Post deleted on July 1, 2009 at 12:59pm

Post deleted on July 1, 2009 at 1:00pm

Post #42

1 reply

You replied to Judy's post on July 1, 2009 at 2:38pm

Criminal Compensation does not give very much, and also given she is making application now and the case is not over, they may not award her anything. Usually they award counselling sessions that kind of thing. I think they also award money in situations where the person was unable to work due to being a victim of the crime, and with TM from what the media reported was on welfare, which means she already wasnt working so I dont believe they will give her anything for nto working.

Delete Post

Post #43

1 reply

Barb Returns (Kitchener, ON) replied to your poston July 1, 2009 at 11:16pm

Thanks Sarah, that gives me hope she'll get nothing which is what she deserves IMO. As a recipient of OW in a household with a second income earner also on OW, they are covered for any of those needs with regard to councelling for any one of the three of them. What more does she want it for?

Post deleted on July 2, 2009 at 12:13am

Post deleted on July 2, 2009 at 12:42am

Post #46

Barb Returns (Kitchener, ON) replied to Julie's poston July 2, 2009 at 12:49am

Thanks for the added information Julie.

Post #47

1 reply

Judy Manzo (Kitchener, ON) replied to Julie's poston July 2, 2009 at 4:01am

Thanks for the info Julie...wasnt aware that they have changed their protocol...which is good for those who deserve it.

I hope when it comes to paying out "pain and suffering" on this case, they really review all the video's ... then they will realize the money for "pain and suffering" will be better paid to someone who deserves it.

Post #49

You replied to Julie's post on July 2, 2009 at 8:42pm

I was a victim of Criminal Harrassment (STALKING) I had to relocate to another city to get away from my offender, I applied for Compensation through the CRIMINAL COMPENSATION BOARD, they only provided me with 12 counselling sessions. They never even reiumbursed me for all my relocation costs etc. Also, my friend two years ago was riding a pedal bike on New Years Eve, and someone was drinking & driving they threw out a beer bottle and it hit her in the back of the head which led to her having a bicycle accident where the handle went through her eye she ended up losing her eye, and now has a glass one and she applied through criminal injury and they didnt give her anything at all,except counselling sessions, and $200 to replace her bike, and $200 for replacing her clothing. So I am truly flabergasted as to how much the Criminal INjury board would actually alot out to people. And if they are calculating hte amounts it costs them to pay for counselling stuff like that.

Post #50

1 reply

You replied to Julie's poston July 2, 2009 at 8:49pm

According to the link you provided it was a 2005 statistical report, average award was $6, 815 also here is who is elgible Who is Eligible for Compensation?

• Individuals who have been injured as a result of a crime of violence committed in Ontario. Examples of a criminal code offence include assault, sexual assault, criminal harassment, etc. Injuries received from a motor vehicle accident (hit and run or drunk driving) are excluded
under the Act, unless the vehicle is used as a weapon

• Individuals that are responsible for the care of a victim of crime and suffered a loss of income or had expenses as a result of the victim's injury or death

• Individuals who are the dependant of a deceased victim (in the case of murder)

• Individuals that were injured while trying to prevent a crime or while helping a police officer make an arrest

In my observation: She was not dependant on the deceased victim as the victim was a child, she did not lose income as she was on welfare, and any expenses she incurred while searching such as phone bills, would be covered by the numerous fund raisers that were conducted. I dont believe they would award her anything under their guidelines, what do you think?

Post #54

1 reply

Barb Returns (Kitchener, ON) replied to Julie's poston July 3, 2009 at 5:19pm

""IMO the only claim she could make is nervous or mental shock you be the judge do you think based on the 2 descriptions of PTSD and ASD she would qualify for compensation?""

Not if the people on the decision panel ever read any of these forums but in all likelihood none of them ever will have ever heard how Tara has behaved. Unfortunate for all the tax payers.

Post deleted on July 3, 2009 at 6:23pm

Post #56

1 reply

Heather Gogan (Halifax, NS) wrote on July 4, 2009 at 6:52pm

what is the rose group??

Post deleted on July 4, 2009 at 7:30pm

Note From Tara Mcdonald

Topic: **Note From Tara Mcdonald**

Displaying all 25 posts by 17 people.

Post #1

Misty Wells wrote on June 27, 2009 at 2:08pm

Today, I was looking at my home page and out of my
corner eye I notice this under "highlights"

Tara McDonald's Notes Tara's

FOR THE F***TARDS.....

Today at 11:11am

SLANDER.......

In law, defamation (also called calumny, libel (for

written words), slander (for spoken words), and vilification) is the communication of a statement that makes a claim, expressly stated or implied to be factual, that may give an individual, business, product, group, government or nation a negative image. It is usually, but not always,[1] a requirement that this claim be false and that the publication is communicated to someone other than the person defamed (the claimant).

In common law jurisdictions, slander refers to a malicious, false and defamatory spoken statement or report, while libel refers to any other form of communication such as written words or images. Most jurisdictions allow legal actions, civil and/or criminal, to deter various kinds of defamation and retaliate against groundless criticism. Related to defamation is public disclosure of private facts, which arises where one person reveals information that is not of public concern, and the release of which would offend a reasonable person. "Unlike

[with] libel, truth is not a defence for invasion of privacy."[2]

Just to make myself clear.....since people use my child's photographs...and speak about myself and my fiancee, my son, and my baby daughter, claiming that they have facts, and can back up their statements with newspaper articles (cause if it's in the papers, it's the God's written truth right?) Well, people better start figuring our where all their links are, and how they can prove what they're saying is the truth......
The only people who need to be investigating are the police.....and when their wasting their time with idiots calling in rediculous information, that's taking their time away from finding my daughter, and slamming these pigs asses to the wall....so please, let them do their job, and leave the investigation to the professionals......

Post #2

2 replies

Barb Returns (Kitchener, ON) wrote on June 27, 2009 at 2:23pm

LOL.. well good for you Tara...you can "CUT and PASTE" but obviously you can't COMPREHEND WHAT YOU HAVE CUT AND PASTED.

Oh, and that will look lovely on your lawsuit:

Plaintiff: Tara McDonald
Defendants: FUC*TARDS from around the internet

Post #3

1 reply

Misty Wells wrote on June 27, 2009 at 2:34pm

I think the ONLY lawsuit she should have against is the newspaper who printed those articles not anyone else. If she didnt think they were the "FACTS" she should of called them or emailed them to tell them that from the start and say hey this isnt true? but why wait until now??? hmmm getting married? tubes untide can this be the reason why she wants to sue someone?

Post #4

Rosie Smart replied to Misty's post on June 27, 2009 at 2:43pm

I doubt she can even Sue anyone. No one has threatened her. Nor Slandered. Nothing that isnt the TRUTH!

She is pissed that she can't do a thing about it that now she is trying to threaten everyone into stopping What???

JMO

Post #5

1 reply

Misty Wells replied to Barb's poston June 27, 2009 at 2:48pm

Barb I like that one *LOL*

Plaintiff: Tara McDonald

Defendants: FUC*TARDS from around the internet

She claiming the pictures are hers well she better sue the news station because they are the ones that put it all over the internet and tv.

Post #6

Rosie Smart replied to Misty's poston June 27, 2009 at 2:50pm

They are not her pictures. They belong to the media and media made them public. She asked the media to be there daily. Those pics are MEDIAS!
Soooo Sorry Tara lol

Post #7

1 reply

Chris Wilson replied to Barb's poston June 27, 2009 at 3:01pm

LMFAO......

(on the stand)

Please raise your right hand Mrs.Fucktard.....do you swear to tell the truth...the whole truth and nothing but the truth so help you god...Mrs.Fucktard"

Post #8

Barb Returns (Kitchener, ON) wrote on June 27, 2009 at 3:08pm

I know... If I were EVERYONE lol...I wouldn't spend 2 seconds out of your valuable time to worry about Tara and her lawsuit bullshit. She doesn't know what she's talking about but she thinks that each time she says the words "lawsuit", "defamation" or "slander" that she's shutting people up b/c she has some power over them. She doesn't. She's grasping at straws and doesn't know what else to do. IMO Tara created this situation in more than one way and now she doesn't know what to do with the FALL OUT that has occurred. Nothing more, nothing less.

Post #9

Diane Ross (St. Catharines / Niagara, ON) wrote on June 27, 2009 at 3:37pm

"Just to make myself clear.....since people use my child's photographs...and speak about myself and my fiancee, my son, and my baby daughter, claiming that they have facts, and can back up their statements with newspaper articles (cause if it's in the papers, it's the God's written truth right?) Well, people better start figuring our where all their links are, and how they can prove what they're saying is the truth......"

is she going to sue the media too then? she's saying the media has their facts wrong as well.

interesting.

Post deleted on June 27, 2009 at 7:08pm

Post deleted on June 27, 2009 at 10:24pm

Post #12

Sue Boyle Goguen (Saint John, NB) wrote on June 29, 2009 at 6:09pm

is TM forgetting that she contributed most of her info to the media..in the first place..

Post #13

Sheila Parker- Westover wrote on June 29, 2009 at 6:32pm

Hey can I be a Fuc tard too?? that sounds like a fun thing to be ! lol

Post #14

Leanne Congdon (London, ON) wrote on June 29, 2009 at 6:33pm

lol its an open title feel free to join us we love being called names ~jokes~

Post #15

Misty Wells wrote on June 29, 2009 at 6:55pm

You cant have my name leanne Tara calls me that lol
she is mainly talking about me and no one else just
to let you know. I told hubby and he just laughed
at her he thinks its ridiculous and she shouldnt be
online if she cant deal with the things being said

Post #16

Leanne Congdon (London, ON) wrote on June 29, 2009
at 7:50pm

@ misty, you can have the name lol,i've been called
worse by more important ppl, but misty remember
sticks and stones could break your bones but stupid
ppl's immature names should never hurt you!!!lol
love this group.ps misty just so there is no hurt
feelings im not in any way trying to insult you.

Post #17

Judy Manzo (Kitchener, ON) wrote on June 29, 2009 at 7:52pm

@ Leanne....

but misty remember sticks and stones could break your bones but stupid ppl's immature names should never hurt you!!!

LMAO..that's a good one

Post #18

Heather Gogan (Halifax, NS) wrote on July 4, 2009 at 6:14pm

i've always been a fuc tard...lol...no one ever tried to sue me because of it... lol

Post #19

Jules Granger replied to Chris's post on July 4, 2009 at 9:22pm

What class, eh...

Post #20

Bryan Farago (Hamilton, ON) wrote on July 4, 2009 at 10:32pm

i already sent this to rosie and i think its funnny we all talk about suspition and how she lies about this and that but we wouldnt say this if it wasnt for how she acts/what she says/or how she makes threats...oh and the lies oh the lies and ive said it before not going to rant but gettin married have another kid doing fuck all but lerking facebook tryin to make sum paper :(:(:(:(

Post #21

Barb Returns (Kitchener, ON) wrote on July 5, 2009 at 2:43am

Yes, it seems to be A LOT about money, doesn't it Bryan?

Post #22

Bryan Farago (Hamilton, ON) wrote on July 5, 2009 at 12:04pm

i think so 100%

Post #23

Joanna Ferri wrote on July 5, 2009 at 1:22pm

waaaaaaaaaaaaaa..boohooo......

and since when has the police ever said this...quoted from Tara the public "... wasting their time with idiots calling in rediculous information"...if it wasn't for the public helping where did the majority of the cules/tips come from????

Post #24

Gaylene Bowman wrote on July 5, 2009 at 4:15pm

MY MY MY Tara rides again. LMAO
Too bad she cant find a more productive way to

spend her time.....like...get a job... Good luck suing Tara..and by the way calling us all Fuc tards has defamed our character...snicker.....should we sue her???? Do

#25

Mark Walters wrote on July 5, 2009 at 8:05pm

she needs to get a job....get a life...stop using the system....so does her fiance as she calls him....maybe we all as taxpayers should sue her for defrauding welfare ...for the last 3 or 4 years....sick of paying for her and her so called fiance as they sit on their asses doing nothing....grow up u 2 and work for your money like the rest of us....stop being Freddie and Freda the free loaders...

Where's Roxxy these days!!Displaying posts 1 - 30 out of 48 by 18 people.

Post #1

Rosie Smart wrote on June 27, 2009 at 11:45am

Hopefully being blood tested! She hasnt been posting on Rose group in days.

Post #2

Chris Wilson wrote on June 27, 2009 at 1:08pm

"Hopefully being blood tested!"
Nice Rosie.

Post #3

1 reply

Barb Returns (Kitchener, ON) wrote on June 27, 2009 at 2:26pm

giggles... I doubt it but it would be nice to get one issue out of the way in this case.

Roxxy and James are the two who fly the lowest beneath the radar...I sure hope that they are being monitored for their whereabouts at all times.

Seriously, She needs tested. To many adoptions and TLM adopted too. And In a fishy way.

Post #5

1 reply

Barb Returns (Kitchener, ON) wrote on June 27, 2009 at 3:12pm

Truly Rosie. I was talking to someone recently (you know who you are) and they said that they don't think that Roxxy can be compelled to take a DNA test against her will. Maybe this is why the case hasn't been just "wrapped up" yet. If that's the case then police or private investigators will have to obtain DNA surreptitiously which might be very difficult if she doesn't smoke or isn't in the habit of drinking out of water bottles or the like where she throws them away publicly.

Post #6

Rosie Smart replied to Barb's poston June 27, 2009 at 3:23pm

I understand, But from my understanding. Police didnt want to go to Roxxy just yet. Because of the Tori case. With MR father having same name as guy in Tania case.

Post #7

Rosie Smart wrote on June 27, 2009 at 4:35pm

Just to weird that she looks So much like Tania

Post deleted on June 27, 2009 at 10:29pm

Post #9

1 reply

Charlotte Beal wrote on June 27, 2009 at 11:02pm

I dont unterstand how if she was 6 when she was taken, that she doesnt remember who she was ? I do believe she is Tania . The pictures tell it all. IMO

Post #10

1 reply

Chris Wilson replied to Charlotte's poston June 29, 2009 at 6:34pm

I agree 100% Charlotte. If she had been 1 or 2....fine........but not 6. A 6yr old is going to know that she has not seen her mother for a while....a 6yr old is going to know that her name is not Tania anymore...a 6 yr old is going to know that she does not have any of her favourite toys anymore.....

I am not saying Roxxy is not Tania......the pictures tell all.

Post #11

1 reply

Lisa Klein-Gunnewiek (Kingston, ON) replied to Chris's post on June 29, 2009 at 6:40pm

I don't remember anything until maybe, like some starts to come back to me around 12 years old. Now a friend of mine remembers from 2 on. Getting a new mommy might be something I would remember but who knows.

Just saying everyone is different.

Post #12

1 reply

Sheila Parker- Westover wrote on June 29, 2009 at 6:41pm

But she could at age 6 be convinced that her mom
gave her to them and brainwashed to belive it was
someone she knew that was Tania not her

Post #13

1 reply

Lisa Klein-Gunnewiek (Kingston, ON) replied to
Sheila's poston June 29, 2009 at 6:43pm

Also Stockholm Syndrome.

Post #14

Dawn Bossert MacEachern wrote on June 29, 2009 at
7:13pm

I can recall from about 3 yrs of age on but only
mostly traumatic things like my dad being very ill
and my pet being hit by a car and then only

vaguely...

Also, Tania couldve been drugged so that would make her not recall accurately too and if she was told certain info enough times, at a young age of 6/7 she would believe it....

Roxxy has fuzzy memories of things....and what need made her post on the Tania site...definitely something there...

Post #15

Dawn Bossert MacEachern replied to Lisa's poston June 29, 2009 at 7:14pm

yep, and most children give unconditional love to their caretakers...

Post #16

Rosie Smart wrote on June 29, 2009 at 8:04pm

Sean Couch (London, ON) wrote

at 9:27pm

There is no cat out of the bag people. The accuasations some of you have made are insane and causing the murrell family more heartach than good. Keyboard detectives make all the good people out there look like complete and total asses. The reason I say this, is because I'm dating your so called Tania, and have spent time with her family. Viewing baby pictures and the usual getting to know you type of thing. As far as the link to Tori Stafford, You obviously have nothing better to do than sit behind your monitors and create drama for the people who really care. Grow up!! Your look a like has already been in contact with the family of Tania, and is deeply disturbed some of you keep posting your false and over imaginative induced theories about the events that took place 27 years ago. To those of you who still have hope, Keep it alive. As we are for Tori.

JUST POSTED ON Elysia's website Help Find Tania Murrell

Funny I knew it wouldnt be Roxxy to respond. Thought it was gonna be Tara not Sean. But the reason I thought that it wouldnt be Roxxy is because some truth to this must be true as she posted almost nightly on Rose group and hasnt since the day we posted about it. Opinions group and this one.

Post #17

1 reply

Dawn Bossert MacEachern wrote on June 29, 2009 at 8:11pm

is Tara a member of the Tania site????? i dont think i saw her name there...

Post #18

1 reply

Rosie Smart replied to Dawn's poston June 29, 2009 at 8:14pm

I dont think so. BUT roxxy add Elsye not elsye added roxxy as a friend.

Hmmmm

Post #19

Dawn Bossert MacEachern replied to Rosie's poston June 29, 2009 at 8:18pm

that is interesting...

Post deleted on June 30, 2009 at 7:00am

Post #21

Dawn Bossert MacEachern replied to Rosie's poston
June 30, 2009 at 8:45am

will be interesting to see what answers you receive
Rosie...i will be watching the site today for
sure....

Post #22

1 reply

Barb Returns (Kitchener, ON) replied to Lisa's
poston June 30, 2009 at 9:42am

""I don't remember anything until maybe, like some
starts to come back to me around 12 years old. Now
a friend of mine remembers from 2 on. Getting a new
mommy might be something I would remember but who

knows.Just saying everyone is different.""

That's a good point Lisa because I never knew that people don't remember stuff in the same way as children. I can remember by brother's birth when I was 2 years and 3 months old and then I can clearly remember my swimming lessons at 2 and a half but that's as far back as I remember things. I really had no idea that other people don't remember things that early. My relatives always laugh at some of the things I remember from long ago past. I always remember stupid little things too like odd clocks that people owned or strange decor in their houses...things like that. Just like whether people remember their dreams too... I'm a vivid dreamer and remember at least 2 or 3 dreams every morning when I wake but I just thought everyone was like that. I was astonished to know so many people don't even remember dreaming at night.

Post #23

Rosie Smart replied to Barb's poston June 30, 2009 at 9:47am

My husband was tramatizes when a child. He remembers nothing much until he hit 30. It happens in dreams now and he wakes crying like achild. I read up on this and it is said that when a child goes through memories that they cant handle or dont want to remember they surpress them and when they are older and dream about things that happened as a child THEY accually feel like they are a child and in that situation all over again.

Post #24

1 reply

Rosie Smart wrote on June 30, 2009 at 9:48am

Just a thought as to why Roxxy says it haunts her dreams.

Post #25

Barb Returns (Kitchener, ON) replied to Rosie's poston June 30, 2009 at 9:56am

I"m sure it does... I'm sure you're right about the similarity between your husband's trauma and Roxxy's.

Post #26

1 reply

Dawn Bossert MacEachern wrote on June 30, 2009 at 9:58am

Just posted by Roxxy on the Tania Murrell site....

Roxxy Knecht (Hamilton, ON) wrote at 12:48pm
further more creating false leads doesn't help to make people aware that Tania is still missing it draws attention away from the fact. if you are

concerned you can print out her age progressed picture make some posters get them out there .. I bid you good day Rosie.

Report

Roxxy Knecht (Hamilton, ON) wrote

at 12:45pm

Good afternoon Rosie , what exactly is it you feel I need to share or prove to you or anyone else for that matter, Because I have Joined groups out of Concern for two Missing individuals.. One who Police Say is no longer with us and the other who is STILL missing. I have been informed of the ludicris theory going around and all I can say to this is you guys are really reaching. and if I really must share My life story with anyone it would only be With Elysia to ease her mind being that I've already done so and she is satisfied as she stated if anyone wants to pay attention to what she has to say . I really have to say this Rosie I find it rather offensive that your speculating" For

Tori" has Brought you to this group to create

further Drama for the Family and Friends of Tania

Murrell. you really should be ashamed of yourself

and apologise

clearly you need a good hobby other then trying to

solve missing persons cases baring that maybe its

time to seek counselling for your obsession

Post #27

Rosie Smart replied to Dawn's poston June 30, 2009

at 9:59am

Rosie Smart wrote

at 12:53pm

Sorry Roxxy it wasnt me that started this Nor let

the cat outta the bag. and as for Elsye...... I say

nothing. I know more than you know. Until I am told

different by (whom I cant say) I will follow my

instincts as I am not blind! Like some people who

have also used these words to.

Post #28

1 reply

Dawn Bossert MacEachern wrote on June 30, 2009 at 10:00am

so Roxxy is definitely reading what is being posted, or someone claiming to be her is...now to hear from Elysia

Post #29

1 reply

Rosie Smart replied to Dawn's poston June 30, 2009 at 10:03am

Yep! I know Elyse has posted this is untrue. But she has too! Also I havent heard different yet. Will let you know if I do.

Post #30

1 reply

Barb Returns (Kitchener, ON) replied to Rosie's poston June 30, 2009 at 10:11am

Has Elysia said it's not true? Or did she only say that the two crimes were not connected? Maybe I missed it and if I did please correct me b/c I only heard that one statement and it certainly doesn't make any denial about Roxxy NOT being Tania. Can you clarify Rosie?

Topic: <u>Where's Roxxy these days!!</u>

<u>Delete Topic</u>|<u>Reply to Topic</u>

Displaying posts 31 - 48 out of 48 by 18 people.

Post deleted on June 30, 2009 at 4:30pm

Post #32

1 reply

<u>Rosie Smart</u> replied to <u>Barb's post</u>on June 30, 2009 at 4:40pm

She said it was not true. On the Tania Murrell wall. But ...

Post deleted on June 30, 2009 at 4:50pm

Post #34

Diane Ross (St. Catharines / Niagara, ON) replied to Rosie's post on June 30, 2009 at 5:01pm

i believe she said the two cases were not connected. she never said anything about roxxy not being tania.

Post #35

1 reply

Diane Ross (St. Catharines / Niagara, ON) wrote on June 30, 2009 at 5:02pm

Elysia Murrell wrote

at 12:40pm on June 25th, 2009

hello everyone

there has been some rumors going around about tania

and the torri casethere is no connetion in the 2

cases i just wanted to clear that up thanks

Post #38

Jules Granger wrote on June 30, 2009 at 6:07pm

Holy F, Rosie

Post #39

Sheila Parker- Westover wrote on June 30, 2009 at
6:55pm

wow no doubt there is there

Post #40

Misty Wells wrote on June 30, 2009 at 7:02pm

HOLY SHIT what a match

Post #41

Judy Manzo (Kitchener, ON) wrote on June 30, 2009 at 7:14pm

wow...no wonder they want you to drop the topic for a bit.

Post #42

Lynn McLeod wrote on June 30, 2009 at 7:50pm

In the photo link posted above was anything other then the hair altered in the photo? If not that is a "CRAZY" match for Tania Murrell. In Crazy I mean they look sooo much alike.

Post #43

Dianna Holden (Vancouver, BC) wrote on June 30, 2009 at 9:22pm

Everyone has a twin out there somewhere, and given Roxxy has responded to the accusations makes me think that perhaps she is not Tania Murrell, although there so many identical marks etc. It seems that a DNA should be done however, chances are it wont happen. JMO

Post #44

Becky Roach replied to Rosie's poston June 30, 2009 at 10:18pm

does that mean we have to drop it too? or just you lol

Post #45

1 reply

Lynn McLeod wrote on July 5, 2009 at 4:38am

Not sure if we are still allowed to comment on this so if my post gets deleted I understand. I did some snooping around and googled Roxxy. I found this on an adoption website she is looking for an older brother think it is from 2000 it ws posted. http://registry.adoption.com/records/67765.html

It does list a name of her another younger brother and I checked out his profile on fb. As much as Roxxy looks like Tania, her and the younger brother look very much alike. It is the older brother she was looking for not to confuse anyone.

Post #46

1 reply

Rosie Smart replied to Lynn's poston July 5, 2009 at 6:15am

Look alike? Yes and no . He has a huge chin and different ears. But the eyes look similar.

Post #47

Lynn McLeod replied to Rosie's poston July 6, 2009 at 1:33pm

Yes I agree maybe it is more the eyes that are similar. I do think she looks more like the Tania Murrell picture but did a see resemblance with the brother. Hopefully time with tell........

Heather Ann Daley-Hall replied to Barb's poston July 6, 2009 at 2:40pm

James was out walking the dog last night....Tara was home also don't think they are going to leave Woodstock, did not see Daryn he was not outside and he was not with James walking the dog, hopefully Rodney or Tara's mom has him at the trailer.....also over 20 cars in parking lot tonight.....

Testify / Married / Common law

Back to Victoria Stafford Group For Those Who Believe There Is More To This CASE!!

Topic: Testify / Married / Common law

Delete Topic|Reply to Topic

Displaying all 26 posts by 8 people.

Post #2

2 replies

Joanna Ferri replied to Rosie's post on July 1, 2009 at 9:33am

Good reads Rosie..once again i`m surfing the web instead of finishing my term peper..grrr...but, I came across this site, not sure if all these terms are considered here in Canada ...so a confession is not admissable..why are they in jail then

``CORPUS DELICTI

"Body of the crime" (Latin). The objective proof that a crime has been committed.

A confession is not admissible if the "corpus" of the crime cannot be proven``

Post #3

Joanna Ferri wrote on July 1, 2009 at 9:43am

Anyone heard of this?

"180 Day Rule

A rule that allows people who are in county jails awaiting trial on felony charges for 180 days to be released on their own recognizance if the delay has not been caused by the accused or the accused's attorney.

A rule that requires all pending charges against a
state prison inmate be brought to trial in 180
days, or be dismissed with prejudice. "

"FELONY
a crime carrying more than one year possible
incarceration."

Post #4

1 reply

Sue Boyle Goguen (Saint John, NB) wrote on July 1,
2009 at 9:46am

is that rule in Canada or U.S.?
@ Joanna..sorry for questioning....

Post #5

Joanna Ferri replied to <u>Sue's post</u>on July 1, 2009 at 10:04am

U.S. .... I was just wondering if anyone heard of this as a Canadian rule??

Post #6

1 reply

You replied to <u>Joanna's post</u>on July 1, 2009 at 2:42pm

thats in the USA not applicable to canada, sorry to point this out :(

Post #7

Joanna Ferri replied to <u>your post</u>on July 1, 2009 at 3:08pm oh don't be sorry, I was wondering if it was the same in canada...thanks for clearing it up :O)

Post #9

Gaylene Bowman wrote on July 2, 2009 at 4:55am

Now correct me if I am wrong but I believe that even if she marries him Ontario Laws state that if the crime was committed when they were not married, getting married will not cause the spouse to be exempt from testifying in court against their husband/wife.

Post #10

Gaylene Bowman wrote on July 2, 2009 at 5:14am

After more reading...sigh...found this in the Canada Evidence Act.

Canada Evidence Act

4. (1) Every person charged with an offence, and, except as otherwise provided in this section, the wife or husband, as the case may be, of the person so charged, is a competent witness for the defence, whether the person so charged is charged solely or jointly with any other person.

Post #11

Barb Returns (Kitchener, ON) wrote on July 2, 2009 at 6:41am

That's for the defence, what about the prosecution?

Post #12

Gaylene Bowman wrote on July 2, 2009 at 3:05pm

OOPs your right..Back to the books...LOL thanks Barb..now your making me read more IMAO

Post #13

Gaylene Bowman wrote on July 5, 2009 at 4:33pm

There it is...Section 235 of the criminal code is the punishment for First degree Murder. So it looks like no matter what they do..they will still be culpible if they were involved.

Offences against young persons

(4) The wife or husband of a person charged with an offence against any of sections 220, 221, 235, 236, 237, 239, 240, 266, 267, 268 or 269 of the Criminal Code where the complainant or victim is under the age of fourteen years is a competent and compellable witness for the prosecution without the consent of the person charged.

Post #14

Lisa Klein-Gunnewiek (Kingston, ON) wrote on July 6, 2009 at 6:00am

I had EXfriends that got married, after the fact, so they could not testify against each other, AND it was murder charges.

Post #15

1 reply

Gaylene Bowman wrote on July 6, 2009 at 11:06am

Lisa

In this case because the crime was against a child under 14 years the law is different as you can see above. If it had been someone over 14 that had been murdered they could have gained an advantage through marriage.

Lisa Klein-Gunnewiek (Kingston, ON) replied to Gaylene's poston July 6, 2009 at 11:08am

How about mentally challenged?

Post #17

Gaylene Bowman wrote on July 6, 2009 at 11:25am

I am not sure about mentally challenged. I am not sure it is even covered in the Criminal Code. I would have to do some more research, but obviously, if they didnt have to testify against each other, they were protected. Sounds very, very sad tho.

Post #20

1 reply

Gaylene Bowman wrote on July 6, 2009 at 3:20pm

@ Julie Very nice research but this is what I have based my info on. It is a less complicated version, backed up by several Chief Justices, Law Societies etc. etc. all trying to have the current laws changed.

My research ULCC (Uniform Law Conference of Canada)
I dont want to get into a long drawn out essay here
so I have only pasted the relevent points brought
before the Conference and what is and what is not
related to this particular case. It is a very
interesting read and can be found at ULCC.ca if you
care to check it out.

It seems to me the more important testimony for
this case would be the evidenciary testimony. Since
the spouse can be forced to testify when children
are involved I believe what they saw in this case
is particularily more important than a confession.

This is the current law:::

The crown can compel a spouse to testify if the
murder victim was 13, but not if the murder victim
was 14

Spouses who witness the murder of a child or a
sexual assault can be forced to reveal what they
saw, but spouses who are the recipient of an
admission of that same crime cannot be forced to
reveal what they heard.

1 reply

Gaylene Bowman wrote on July 6, 2009 at 3:52pm

Exactly ...and that is what I was trying to convey.
:)

So far as a confession goes...that would be correct. How would one know??

Answer not admissible against witness:

(2) Where with respect to any question a witness objects to answer on the ground that his answer may tend to criminate him, or may tend to establish his liability to a civil proceeding at the instance of the Crown or of any person, and if but for this Act, or the Act of any provincial legislature, the witness would therefore have been excused from answering the question, then although the witness is by reason of this Act or the provincial Act compelled to answer, the answer so given shall not

be used or admissible in evidence against him in any criminal trial or other criminal proceeding against him thereafter taking place, other than a prosecution for perjury in the giving of that evidence or for the giving of contradictory evidence.

Hope that covers your questions. I agree about the criminal code but my answers are mostly in this case from the Canada Evidence Act. :)

Post #24

Gaylene Bowman wrote on July 7, 2009 at 5:15am

What the above states is that in a case where you as a witness are compelled to answer, the answer you give shall not be used against you in a criminal proceeding thereafter. So it does not say you wont have to answer the question (depending on the laws) just that if you do, it cant be later used as evidence against you.

When is this helpful. Certainly not if both spouses

are involved in a crime. When it is helpful is if one spouse has seen a crime comitted by the other spouse or has information relevent to the crime, other than an admission of guilt by the spouse.

Post #25

1 reply

Gaylene Bowman wrote on July 7, 2009 at 5:27am

A good point in this is (a child under 14 as applied by the law) is murdered and one spouse is forced to testify against the other. Spouse 1 testifies that Spouse 2 strangled the child. While it does incriminate Spouse 1 for accessory to murder, it is not neccesarily the evidence that the crown would need to make an accessory to murder charge stick. So the testimony of Spouse 1 would be helpful to get a conviction against Spouse 2, yet it would not hurt the case against Spouse 1. Perhaps a bit of a simple explanation but basically how I see it.

Of course this is simply my interpretation of how I see it explained in the ULCC along with what the Canada Evidence Act establishes.

Topic: <u>does anyone remember</u>

Post #1

<u>Paula StPierre</u> (London, ON) wrote on July 20, 2009 at 8:23am

does anyone remember the pyschic sinclair that use to do up drawings that he said Tori was showing him.. i remember he did a drawing that looked like a face sort of indian face.. look at this http://www.thespec.com/News/BreakingNews/article/60 3139 right near where they found the remains.. the shape of lake simcoe!!

Post #2

Paula StPierre (London, ON) wrote on July 20, 2009
at 8:38am

never mind they changed they picture so you cant
see it

Post #3

Paula StPierre (London, ON) wrote on July 20, 2009
at 8:43am

TELEPHONE INTERVIEW WITH KAYLA HURST

Back to Victoria Stafford Group For Those Who
Believe There Is More To This CASE!!Post #1

2 replies

Dianna Holden (Vancouver, BC) wrote on July 13,
2009 at 9:55pm

PLEASE NOTE: THIS LINK is graphic and please dont play with little ears near by. LISTENER DISCRETION IS ADVISED and this is very GRAPHIC.

Furthermore, THIS HAS NOTHING TO DO WITH ME, OR MY AGENCY, I recorded this because I was hoping it could provide some answers but what came out of this interview I believe was more deception and lies, however I believe there was some truth to it.

http://www.ustream.tv/recorded/1805452

This is part 1 of 2 part 2 is not uploaded as of yet. I do not endorse anything that is said in the conversation nor do I agree with what was said.

Post #2

Rosie Smart replied to Dianna's poston July 13, 2009 at 9:57pm

She has way to many holes and conderdicts herself way to much . I call Lier! She is full of it IMO I think Rod needs to charge her ass!

Post #3

Jennifer Etsell (Kitchener, ON) wrote on July 14, 2009 at 5:16am

Does she know that she was being recorded

Post #4

Gaylene Bowman wrote on July 14, 2009 at 5:38am

That is pretty crazy, but..I hope you told her you were recording the conversation.
Take it with a grain of salt. I do believe she is likely exagerating the truth because Dianna is her new friend she is trying to impress. No doubt she will be getting a visit from the cops after this conversation gets out. It wont be on You Tube for

long is my guess. If she knew you were recording Dianna, nice work. If she didnt I dont know what to say. WOW!! If she was alive for 4 or 5 hours that will not be good for the local police. Very sad indeed.

Post #5

Jennifer Etsell (Kitchener, ON) wrote on July 14, 2009 at 5:41am

I don't know what to say. she sounds cracked out.

Post #6

1 reply

Jennifer Etsell (Kitchener, ON) wrote on July 14, 2009 at 5:49am

he hates kids???? not to my knowledge. Dianna good for you?? you stayed so neutral. Court date??? There is a court date for Michael this friday and one for Terri Lynn in Aug. Is she really talking to Terri?? oh and there are no incoming calls that go to inmates in jail. The inmates can only making outside calls and they have to be collect.

Post #7

Rosie Smart replied to Jennifer's poston July 14, 2009 at 5:56am

Thats right Jennifer and that is just one of the holes in Kaylas story and one of the reasons I say shes full of shit!

Post #8

Jennifer Etsell (Kitchener, ON) wrote on July 14, 2009 at 5:57am

did you see her profile she looks like a quack

Post #9

Jennifer Etsell (Kitchener, ON) wrote on July 14, 2009 at 5:58am

discovery with this Kayla girl. Here is her profile page,

1 reply

Jennifer Etsell (Kitchener, ON) wrote on July 14, 2009 at 6:08am

how much of that conversation is missing??? what was talked about after that??? anything of interest

Post #11

Rosie Smart replied to Jennifer's poston July 14, 2009 at 6:12am

I havent heard all of the first one yet. But I do know it was said that a threeway with Kayla and TLm was gonna be made today to Dianna. BUT Dianna doesnt believe she will as she was supposed to call her last night when Carol got to her house.

Also that fb girl to me doesnt look like the Kayla hurst in this video near the end with Carol either?

Post #12

Jennifer Etsell (Kitchener, ON) wrote on July 14, 2009 at 6:18am

it doesn't look like her but it does sound like her

Post #13

Lynn McLeod wrote on July 14, 2009 at 6:54am

I was think of she is in the meth program weight gain, plus in her fb pic her she has bangs which would make her look different. I agree Jennifer the voice sounds the same. It is pretty clear on the interview with Dianna she doesn't know as much as she maybe let on. I believe a lot of answers were made up.

Post #14

1 reply

Lynn McLeod wrote on July 14, 2009 at 7:07am

Is this posted somewhere else? How would they have it on the discussion board?

Post #15

Rosie Smart replied to Lynn's post on July 14, 2009 at 7:29am

It was on opionions but Kimberly deleted it.

And there are spies in here. I just dont know nor care anymore who they are. But the group still remains private so that all of tara friends cant find it and click on report as I will lose my group again.

Post #16

1 reply

Lisa Klein-Gunnewiek (Kingston, ON) replied to Rosie's poston July 14, 2009 at 7:33am

You mean Diane put the link to the phone conversation on Kimberly's group and she deleted it?
Does anyone know who is yelling at a kid in the background?

Post #17

Rosie Smart replied to Lisa's poston July 14, 2009 at 7:36am

because of the type of phone call Dianna was trying to get her kids to be quite. And she had to play the call in order to upload it. So you will hear back ground noise too.

Post #18

Rosie Smart wrote on July 14, 2009 at 8:45am

Becky Mitchell Wigand (London, ON) wrote at 11:43am

So why is her profile pic Jessica McDonald's pic, it is the same girl from the newspaper Right? Something not right here, Jeanette did you see these questionable posts yourself?

Post #19

Lisa Klein-Gunnewiek (Kingston, ON) replied to Rosie's poston July 14, 2009 at 8:51am

She also sounds like the same person.

Post #20

Lisa Klein-Gunnewiek (Kingston, ON) replied to Dianna's poston July 14, 2009 at 11:08am

Dianna, why did you post this? If you are trying to get information to finding Tori I don't see how plastering this on FB is helping? Did you give a copy to the police? What was the cheque for you sent her and how much was it? Give an addict money they will say anything you want them to.

Post #21

Rosie Smart replied to Lisa's poston July 14, 2009
at 11:53am

I didnt offer her money and she messaged me with
very detailed info.

Post #22

Rosie Smart wrote on July 14, 2009 at 11:54am

Info that I didnt believe for a minute either. To
many holes once again

Post #23

Lisa Klein-Gunnewiek (Kingston, ON) replied to
Rosie's poston July 14, 2009 at 12:02pm

Huh? I was asking Dianna.

Post #24

Rosie Smart replied to Lisa's poston July 14, 2009
at 12:06pm

I know that. I was just saying that I didnt offer her money and she messaged me with stuff. So her talking had nothing to do with money IMO

Post #25

Lisa Klein-Gunnewiek (Kingston, ON) replied to Rosie's poston July 14, 2009 at 12:41pm

Oh!! The whole this is stupid. I see it's gone now anyway. Some people downloaded it of course.

Post #27

Lisa Klein-Gunnewiek (Kingston, ON) replied to Julie's poston July 14, 2009 at 1:10pm

The first half is gone and now you have to PM Dianna H to get the full version. Plus she has to add you as a friend on Ustream or some stupid thing.

post #29

Dianna Holden (Vancouver, BC) replied to Lisa's poston July 14, 2009 at 1:27pm

For starters, I never paid her anything I offerred too because she wouldnt talk to me other wise. Secondly, the complete interview is now posted, thirdly, yes I have made the police aware of this, and fourthly I posted this for the simple reason is this , Although I dont believe this women and the entirty of what she has informed me however, I believe some of what she has stated may be true and some details she provided seems like she was there first hand, but I posted it because maybe someones memory will be jogged if someone on here knows kayla, and they will go forward to police with their own info. Also, I am not "LOOKING" for Tori, I am Not an investigator, I am not a police officer, and I am not involved whatsover in any part of the investigation. I am strictly a civilian who happens to own a people locating agency and is highly interested in this case. That is it.

Post #30

Frances Clarke wrote on July 14, 2009 at 2:33pm

Its gone!!! what happened

<u>Back to Victoria Stafford Group For Those Who
Believe There Is More To This CASE!!</u>

Topic: <u>TELEPHONE INTERVIEW WITH KAYLA HURST</u>

Post #31

Lynn McLeod wrote on July 14, 2009 at 2:45pm

Dianna I don't think you have to explain or defend
yourself here. Great job!!

Post #32

Gaylene Bowman wrote on July 14, 2009 at 3:15pm

Dianna

You may have gotten some useful information and as
I suspected you notified police and now the post is
gone. They will want to review it and decide if
anything is helpful to their case. Conversations
between this girl and TLM may be just the thing
they need and I wouldnt doubt that this girl is now

going to become the OPP's new best friend. There may be details no one else knows about in the conversation, other than TLM, as things have been very tight lipped to date about evidence. Nice work in my opinion. You are a gutsy lady.

Post #33

Lisa Klein-Gunnewiek (Kingston, ON) replied to Dianna's post on July 14, 2009 at 3:15pm

So you promised a young addict who has personal problems money for her to tell you a story? The police won't pay her so she tells someone, something who will pay her? You give me a cheque and I will talk to you!!

Did you go looking for her or did she come looking for you?

Why would you believe anything from someone you have to pay? You obviously lied to her so why would she believe you now and why would you ask her to call you back after you posted this all over the Internet?

You chose to pick out the truth in her story to suit... who?

I seem to have more questions then answers after all this.

Post #34

1 reply

Sue Boyle Goguen (Saint John, NB) wrote on July 14, 2009 at 3:45pm

Dianna..not to take anything from your determinedness..
however, you stated at the beginning of the convo that a cheque was in the mail..you also have stated your agency in that convo..I would like to think that you intend to come good with the money for that girl..she spoke with you on the assumption

that you would compensate her..it would not sit well with any prospective clients if they find you renege on your word..JMO..

Post #35

Patricia Wright wrote on July 14, 2009 at 8:57pm

dianna add me as a friend so i can see a link please

Post #37

Sue Boyle Goguen (Saint John, NB) wrote on July 15, 2009 at 8:06am

@ Julie..ten grand..dunno
@ Dianna..no disrespect meant to you..didnt mean to sound harsh..was just stating my opinion..
I know that KH opened herself to this by agreeing to talk for a sum of money..I just sort of feel bad for her if she finds she was duped and that her convo was displayed in groups for alot of people to see..I know it is not the fault of this group if someone copys and posts on another group..but I

personally would be upset to see a convo I assumed was private being discussed on other forums..

Post #38

Robin Tillmanns replied to Sue's post on July 15, 2009 at 9:03am

Ditto!!! (Except for the determinedness...it came across as obnoxious...if you ask a question, let a person

Post #39

Lynn McLeod wrote on July 15, 2009 at 10:42am

Maybe Dianna's way of getting Kayla to talk wasn't the best choice by offering her money. Then again I would not feel sorry for Kayla if she doesn't receive the money, I think only talking for money shows what kind of person she is.

One thing is everyone on the boards have been wondering about this Kayla and what she had to say. Dianna recorded the conversation and gave everyone what they have wanted to know if this Kayla really knew what she was talking about or not.

Post #40

1 reply

Mark Walters wrote on July 15, 2009 at 1:54pm

wish i could hear the conversation that everyone is talking about...Kayla is a strange girl...wouldnt take too much what she says as the gospel...

Post #41

Heather Ann Daley-Hall replied to Mark's post on July 15, 2009 at 4:29pm

i wouldn't believe anything she is saying, as she is an addict and is going to meth clinic, lost her kids.....not working......hangs out with Carol.....so I would not believe anything she has to say.........JMO

Post #42

Mark Walters wrote on July 15, 2009 at 4:48pm

so true heather ...

Post #43

1 reply

Misty Wells wrote on July 15, 2009 at 6:26pm

Wanted: Need a 2 bedroom apartment asap

Price: Please contact Ad ID: 142148572

Visits: 63

Bathrooms (#): 1 bathroom

Pets Allowed: Yes

Address: Woodstock, ON, N4S 1K5

Date Listed: 14-Jul-09

My girlfriend and I are looking to share an
apartment as we are both needing out of the
situations we are in right now. My boyfriend has
become very verbal and emotional and mentally
abusive and my friends neijbours have been
threatening and harassing her and even the landlord

so we are in need of a 2 bedroom apartment right away... so if you can please contact me that would be great...***-***-****

could it be Carol that she is getting an apartment with?

Post #44

Rosie Smart replied to Misty's post on July 15, 2009 at 8:21pm

Yes that is her. Same number I google that .

Post #45

Dianna Holden (Vancouver, BC) replied to Lynn's post on July 15, 2009 at 11:15pm

Picked yours to reply too Lynn cause so many have questions. First of all I have full intentions of sending Kayla payment, however, its only because I promised that I would, Also I dont believe half of what she informed me during the conversation. IN fact I think she is full of it. I did send the conversation to the police because some of what she told me really sat uneasy with me, at certain times of the conversation, she starts to say "I" then changes it to Terry LYnn said this. It is very concerning to me. So all I can say is this, some people may disagree with the fact that I recorded this, however, I think that it is important, because if people know about kayla etc, they can call police with their own tips. I think Kayla had something to do with something she knows stuff she shouldnt, and I highly doubt TLM told her MR made her shit her pants. Thats a very embarrasing issue so I doubt shed say it, Also, the police would have told Kayla to not talk to anyone, but here she was blabbing to me. And for the person that posted the comment about "How my clients would feel if I didn't pay this person" It is completely irrelevant", as I am hired to locate people by my clients and all they care about is me finding the people.

Post #46

Jennifer Etsell (Kitchener, ON) wrote on July 16, 2009 at 5:58am

Dianna when you took it to the police what did they have to say?? anything?? maybe tomorrow we will find out some more as MR goes to court but I highly doubt it. Kayla didn't even know when TLM went back to court if she is such good friends with her she would know this. I agree that I think she has more to do with it then she is letting on

Post #47

Heather Ann Daley-Hall replied to Jennifer's post on July 16, 2009 at 7:46am

what a town we live in.....they should do a survey to see how many people are addicted to oxys and are getting treatment at the meth clinic, would be interesting to see.......I agree if Terry Lynn was such a good friend she would know that she has another court appearance coming up, also she sees Terry Lynn's mother for sure she would definitly know that her daughter would be going to court, but maybe not if they are all wired out on their drugs......JMO

Post #48

Jennifer Etsell (Kitchener, ON) wrote on July 16, 2009 at 8:13am

ya I just don't know still something weird going on IMO

Post #49

Bryan Farago (Hamilton, ON) wrote on July 16, 2009 at 9:35am

if TLM has been talking to her from jail all that is recorded so the police would have everything they have talked about ????? wouldnt they???????

Post #50

Jennifer Etsell (Kitchener, ON) wrote on July 16, 2009 at 10:29am

I don't know if they can record your conversations from jail. I know there are guards sitting there pretty much listening in on your conversation

Post #51

Heather Ann Daley-Hall wrote on July 16, 2009 at 2:27pm

why wouldn't they be able to record the conversations, they are convicts...why should they have any rights if they commited crimes.....us tax payers get to foot the bill for them, by rights they have no rights when they get locked up...glad im not in power.....things would sure be different......IMO free telephone, free room and board....free tv.....makes me mad.....

Post #53

Heather Gogan (Halifax, NS) wrote on July 20, 2009 at 10:18am all calls are recorded and the inmates are told that they are...I had a bf in the pen before so I know this much...for sure for Nova Scotia anyway...pretty sure it would be the same all over....

Topic: <u>Necklace, does anyone know?</u>

Displaying all 5 posts by 3 people.

Post #1

Vangie Nobbs Alexander (London) wrote on July 22, 2009 at 6:38am

Just a shot in the dark here, but as the saying goes, hidden in plain view.

Does anyone know if Tori was wearing her necklace with the gold heart the day she went missing? The one TM was wearing in the pc's.

Post #2

Monique Breier wrote on July 22, 2009 at 8:48am

Good question?? Because if Tori was wearing it and then Tara was pictured after wards with it on....??????

Post #3

Vangie Nobbs Alexander (London) wrote on July 22, 2009 at 8:49am

would be interesting to find out wouldn't it!!!!

Post #4

Vangie Nobbs Alexander (London) wrote on July 22, 2009 at 11:21am

It's not going to fresh in any one's memory. Those were the only ones I could think of too, other than Daryn, but I would leave that up to family to ask him.

Post #5

Charlotte Beal wrote on July 22, 2009 at 8:22pm

Yes for sure

Post #8

Charlotte Beal wrote on July 21, 2009 at 11:34pm

Oh , I see , she is too distraught to speak right now.

Post #9

Vangie Nobbs Alexander (London) wrote on July 22, 2009 at 5:30am

Is it distraught or fear now that Tori has been found?

Post #10

Charlotte Beal wrote on July 22, 2009 at 10:26am

One or the other , only toris body MAY hold the answers.

Post #11

Bryan Farago (Hamilton, ON) wrote on July 22, 2009 at 2:40pm

FEAR 100% cuz she wasnt showing shit the whole time or maybe its distraught because it shouldnt have happened this way IMO

Post #12

Monique Breier wrote on July 23, 2009 at 5:17am

We can only pray that justice prevails and that the scene where Tori was found holds some other answers. The profiler who found her said he was following some tips and that is how he decided to go down that road....who was tipping him off of her whereabouts???

Displaying all 29 posts by 11 people.

wrote on July 25, 2009 at 6:20am

TLM confessed. She told police a profile place of rocks etc. Tori was found the other direction same profile of an area.

Now what I dont get is TLM and MR were seen in HD in guelph?

Police said they had a strong case and we seen them take evidence from Fergus area.

So what I dont get is how can all that evidence in Fergus be helpful? I mean what evidnce could it be because they took Tori in the oppisite direction.

Okay and if MR moved Tori once TLM was in Jail. Why to a place the same as TLM described?

They either have picture/video or they were lying about a stong case. But I cant see that with 700MB of evidence?

Post #2

Lisa Klein-Gunnewiek (Kingston, ON) wrote on July 25, 2009 at 7:46am

Who knows when they put Tori there? They say they know about the time of her death but did not say what time or even what day they put her in her resting place.

Maybe the Fergus stuff was the shovel etc as to throw police off the trail to another area?

Who the H#!! knows at this point. There is a "rumour" and only rumour that there is video evidence.

Post #3

Monique Breier wrote on July 25, 2009 at 8:09am

Fuck how dumb can you be videoing this crime??? Didn't they at least learn from the likes of Paul and Karla. What would be the purpose of the video.....it's not like they have committed these types of crimes before and need to keep diaries??

Post #4

2 replies

Janet Hall wrote on July 25, 2009 at 8:25am

What I dont understand is if they have video ,
would they not have told MR that they have this and
that they there was no chance of getting out of
this, I am sure they would played TLM against MR
especially before Tori was located just to bring
her back, ok I get that MR might have thought that
Tori would never be located then he possibly would
have thought that the case would have been harder
to prove against him but it wouldnt be hard if this
video existed and you would think he would realize
that.

Maybe I watch too much CSI and Law and Order but
IMO the cops would have done anything to bring her
home and if this video or pictures are really true
I am sure MR would have done what he could to try
and cut a deal before TLM.

I know all this has probably already been said.

Post #5

Rosie Smart replied to Janet's post on July 25, 2009 at 9:10am

Very true.

Post #6

Lisa Klein-Gunnewiek (Kingston, ON) replied to Janet's post on July 25, 2009 at 10:25am

Neither one of them have anything to loose going to trial. Hell, OJ is guilty as sin but got off. Video ~IF THERE IS ONE~ could be deemed inadmissible, too grainy, no faces, no proof of death - really just about anything. A good lawyer can do just about anything.

TYM did talk first. She was helping them and MR lawyer told him to not open his mouth, even to him!! We have to prove him guilty, not him to prove innocence.

I just hope our government is better than their lawyers!!

Post #7

Bryan Farago (Hamilton, ON) wrote on July 25, 2009 at 11:41am

i got in trouble a while back and they told me when i was arrested they have video evidence this and that and they where talking out of ther ass police are allowed to lie and they do it alot

Post #8

Monique Breier wrote on July 25, 2009 at 1:05pm

This is very true Bryan. The police will use strong arm tactics to see if the individual will crumble under pressure....they may have been doing just this to see who spilled first.

Post #9

Gaylene Bowman wrote on July 25, 2009 at 3:33pm

I agree with everything being said above re evidence problems.

IMO if the police had solid video or pic evidence implicating MR he would have plead out and avoided a trial that would expose every dirty pathetic thing he did to that poor child. After all a guilty plea would have allowed sentencing to be immediate, it would not have changed any outcome (if he was guilty) and he would never have had to divulge publicly the details of his crime, or take the chance of every detail coming out via evidence and TLM.

If I was his mother I wold certainly have advised him to admit his guilt, if he was guilty, to avoid all of the above, and avoid all of the negative publicity, and minimize the damage to his families reputation, as well as allow the victims family not to have public the details about the crime that would be difficult for them to bear. As a mother or grandmother she must be very heartbroken and I believe she knows if he is guilty or not.. So far this has not happened which in my mind puts a spin on what is going on.

The police may not have a solid case, and the case may be built in general from statements made by TLM. That could be very risky for the police to go to trial on. After all who really is going to believe what TLM says on the stand. IMO she herself is a pathetic liar that will not make a good witness for the crown. Where is this case going??? That is the question. I just hope the police and crown are very careful with deal making. They may be getting scammed by TLM and MR or just TLM trying to get herself out of a lengthy sentence when she herself is guilty of much more.

Post #10

Judy Manzo (Kitchener, ON) wrote on July 25, 2009 at 9:17pm

Rosie ... what I am having a hard time with is this, if the police have not confirmed that they were able to locate Tori's body by the information that they were given from TLM .... what gives her lawyer the right to state that they are going for a plea bargain.... does this lawyer know something that we havent heard from the police.

I understand that the police are being careful with the information that they are going to give to the media/public. But, if they are hinting at the fact that this was a tip ... why would that lawyer state this

Post #11

Sue Boyle Goguen (Saint John, NB) wrote on July 26, 2009 at 3:29am

if there is recorded evidence of a crime commited by MR, then that should blow TLM's statement about walking away out of the water..someone had to be recording it..

am assuming the evidence would be on a cell..
dunno..

and I agree with Rosie..if MR moved the body, after
TLM was incarcerated, then her description of said
place was a coincidence?..cant figure that one
out..

Post #12

1 reply

Charlotte Beal wrote on July 28, 2009 at 6:30am

My thought on that is that her body was always
there . TLM just got confused as to the exact
location ,if she didint know the area. One fields
with rocks and trees could easily look like another
.The same landmarks were there as the first place
she looked . -rock pile, trees, ... I do wonder
some about that because of the police saying new
tips helped them as well to find her body . She
could have remembered something else recently
though . I do agree that if the public were

informed of all the landmarks to look for her body
might have been found earlier . On the other hand,
maybe if it wasnt TLM that gave the new tips then
more might come of something else the new lead
might have said also and uncover more of this
case,never know .If I had lived in that direct area
and was to have heard about a long dirt driveway ,
that spot would come to mind -no problem .Most
definately the neighbors across the road would
start to wonder EVERY time they walked out the
front door , IMO

Post #13

Rosie Smart replied to Charlotte's post on July 28,
2009 at 8:45pm

Okay but didnt TLM see any signs? Like Mount
Forest! Just dont get it.

Post #14

Charlotte Beal wrote on July 28, 2009 at 10:52pm

Too high or too dark out or the comblination maybe?

Post #15

Charlotte Beal wrote on July 28, 2009 at 10:55pm

my guess is knew she was in Guelph and Furgus but didnt know what way they went after furgus

1 reply

Charlotte Beal wrote on July 29, 2009 at 1:23am

oopps Fergus.

Post #17

Dianna Holden (Vancouver, BC) replied to Charlotte's post on August 9, 2009 at 6:26pm

The best thing to do is if your charged with a serious crime, people tend to plead not guilty, reason being is there is a small chance that there would be an error in law that would get them off, and in canada you cant be tried for the same crime twice, so if he gets off they can appeal it however, it can still prevent him from going to jail. In any event I am pretty certain he is innocent. Not 100 percent however, as its now been 5 months since this horrific ordeal began and the individuals whom I thought was responsible for this crime have not been arrested as of yet

Post #18

Charlotte Beal wrote on August 12, 2009 at 9:04pm

I dont think I really know ANYTHING anymore . I used to have ALOT of different theories of what I thought MIGHT have happened , but now I am unsure of any of them or anyone elses. I just want time to go faster to find out what happened for real.

Post #19

Gaylene Bowman wrote on September 2, 2009 at 12:33pm

Just suppose they had only her word against his, no real evidence and everything is hingeing on DNA evidence and physical evidence found at the crime scene (s) assuming there could possibly be more than one crime scene. What if there is no other evidence other than her statement? Certainly this case could take many twists and turns before trial. It is going to become very interesting in the months to come. Stay tuned because I have a feeling it is going to be one hell of a roller coaster ride!!

Post #21

Dianna Holden (Vancouver, BC) wrote on September 30, 2009 at 10:48pm

Just to advise Rosie, Taras book is about to come out about this whole thing, she signed a deal with someone out of Ontario. Its being sold at Chapters Bookstore.

Post #22

Barb Wagner (London, ON) wrote on October 6, 2009 at 3:53am

What book is that Dianna? Do you have a title?

Post #23

Gaylene Bowman wrote on October 6, 2009 at 4:55am

I have heard some pretty horiffic so called details of the crime scene. All heresay of course but if they are true I would classify this crime as a very horrible one. Whomever killed this child was indeed very sick if anything I have heard is true. At the very least this person (s) have (had) the makings of becoming a serial killer.This was not a mistake. It was cold, calculated and planned. Has anyone else heard any stories via grapevine???? Just my opinion based on second hand information.

Post #25

Barb Wagner (London, ON) wrote on October 8, 2009 at 10:42am

Gaylene...what could have been horrific about the crime scene (if indeed the site they found her body WAS the crime scene and not just a dump site)? A

259

child's body in the elements the length of time
Tori's was out there would be nothing but bones and
a smattering of dried soft tissues. The clothing
may or may not have helped to hold the bones
together in one place and hair would have still
been visible, possibly soughed off from the skull
or still attached by dried tissue but there
shouldn't have been anything particularly
"horrific" about the site. What did you hear?

Post #26

Gaylene Bowman wrote on October 8, 2009 at 3:02pm

What I heard was not so much about the actual crime
scene per say but some of the evidence they
supposedly have. How much of anything we hear is
true or not remains to be seen and I take eveything
I hear with a grain of salt as everyone should. I
have heard that they have video evidence, and that
it is very detailed. This was stated by someone I
dont know and I got the feeling that the person may

have been trying to elevate thier social importance so I am very cautious about taking it to be gospel. The person was pretty detailed and for that reason I was weary of what was said. I think I was also shocked by what was being said. The person didnt say anything about there being anything more that you descibed Barb, just the description of how the remains were found, the state of clothing etc.

Post #27

Charlotte Beal wrote on October 9, 2009 at 10:32pm

Hi, Barb. How are you ? I remember you from the summer with posts. I find you level headed and to the point . Hope you are fine .

Post #28

Barb Wagner (London, ON) wrote on October 13, 2009 at 3:21pm

I'm good Charlotte...thanks for asking....just moved and finding the unpacking and cleaning of the new place quite daunting :o)

Happy Thanksgiving everyone! Hope you had a nice weekend and feasted well on the Turkey-bird ;o)

Post #29

Charlotte Beal wrote on October 20, 2009 at 8:38pm

Yes , we had a good thanks giving . I am so much waiting for the court case on Tori to happen . I also hope there will be 1000 people sign the petitions . AFTER these 2 go to court and found guilty (i , and most think they are)I would like these to be in place. They would not get off so easy -like Carla and Paul. Moving and cleaning and putting away and arranging ....and rearranging and then having to clean again ... NO THANKS.

END OF POSTS FROM THE GROUP .

CHAPTER 7
"Convicted Online"

As you can see from the pages before many people voiced an opinion of what they felt occurred in the Victoria Stafford abduction and murder. Some felt that Tara McDonalds friend Sara Leeper, looked like the police sketch, and was the unidentified women who snatched Victoria from her school. Others thought that Tara McDonald herself took Tori from school. People had their minds made up as to who they thought was guilty.

One individual even had a previous allegation brought up that he was exonerated of years previously, but because he was accused of such a horrific crime against a child, people ignored the publication ban and posted a subpoena of the initial charge sheet. Again police agencies did nothing to have this charge sheet removed from the internet, although there was a court order banning the publication, as it could potentially identify the accuser in the case.

What society didn't realize that with all the rumors and speculations a lot of people got hurt. The things that occurred in the Facebook forums, was absolutely crazy. People were attacking others with their words, posting information from their real lives outside the internet for those to see, all because they were angry that this person said this, that person said that. No one stopped to realize that hang on a second these people had families and that their actions could be putting others in danger. No one knows what kind of lunatics hang out on the boards that discussed the murder and abduction of a child.

Not only was Tara McDonald convicted by society of being involved with her daughters murder, so was her partner James Goris. One might as why society would blame the mother and stepfather of such a horrendous ordeal. It first began with the timeline.

One of the biggest issues people had was the length of time from when Victoria went missing to the time she was reported missing. There was a 3 hour gap, prior to the authorities being notified. Many members of society thought that this was too long of a time period to wait before notifying police that you eight year old is missing.

What about the comments that supposedly the birthmother had stated, again were these fact or were they fiction, after-all, who really knows if she actually told her ex-partner that she hoped that Victoria wasn't missing when he called to inform her he was running late to pick her up for the visit. Again is it rumor or speculation. It certainly would not have been the first time that the public took something small and twisted it.

Then there was the first account of the birthmother claiming she had never done drugs since high school, then admitting that yes she did drugs but she was on the provinces methadone program.

Many people viewed this as ok she's hiding this what else is she hiding. Could it have been just a simple case that she wasn't on trial here? She was trying to find her daughter, perhaps she felt that if the public knew of her previous addiction that maybe no one would help her find her daughter. She didn't want anything hindering her search for her daughter.

Perhaps, another reason Tara McDonald did not want the world to know that she battled a drug addiction, is that it would fuel the rumor that her daughter was missing because of a presumed drug debt.

Ms. McDonalds, credibility began to have its issues. Many of the credibility issues began when she was seen partying it up while the search of her daughter was continuing, with conflicting reports in the media of certain key elements to the case such as whether or not she had a relationship with the two suspects that are accused in her daughters murder and abduction.

Firstly, she claimed that she did not know them, then she stated that she did know them. Conflictions in stories really attack a persons credibility. Many people started wondering when she didn't show emotion to the cameras that were there day in and day out to keep her daughters case in the front lines of the media. Some thought it was strange the way she behaved, through her lack of emotion and the verbal statements that she was making.

Many people handle grief differently, that's what makes people unique in society. When one person may express it outwardly with anger, another may handle it with tears, and others may show no emotion at all because their body completely shuts down. Its not apparent as to what category Ms. McDonald fell into however, regardless of the fact that it appeared to society that she was showing no emotion, who was society to judge that?

Are we that much of a sick and twisted society that we actually wanted this women to pour her heart out to us? Did we want to see her pain and her grief.

Who made us the judge and jury in this case? Even with the opinions of a variety of people, the facts were still there. We were provided with a scenario, of a little girl who went missing, later to be found murdered and two suspects arrested for that murder. So why continue to look into the matter? Why is it that people are so desperate to believe that there is more to it.

Is it because of all the conflicting news stories that we have read or seen on television about this case?. Granted there were numerous contradictory stories, but maybe they were only contradictory because of how they were brought to the attention of the public eye in the first place. You know the way the media portrayed them.

We all so desperately wanted answers, but perhaps over time we will get those answers. Let us take a look at the other people that were accused of involvement in this horrifying ordeal. James Goris for example, a loving partner to Tara McDonald, a loving step father, who stepped up to the plate and helped raise a blended a family. Mr. Goris, rarely talked to the media, perhaps it was because he wasn't photogenic or despised cameras, or perhaps he felt that it would be better if he was just there to support his partner.

The speculations that were speculated about Mr. Goris's involvement in his stepdaughters murder and abduction, were absolutely absurd. People accused Mr. Goris of being involved with a biker gang, however, just for a second even if he was, gangs don't hurt young children, that's only in the movies.

James may have been guilty of loving his stepchildren too much, but he certainly had not been found guilty in a court of law with offences against children, or with respect to being involved in gang activity.

Society, tried and convicted both Tara McDonald & James Goris, with respect to the murder & abduction of Victoria Stafford. Who gives society that right? Individuals have the rights to their opinions, whether they are negative or positive, but to go on a public website where the world can see and post theories after theories, and speculation after speculation about individuals whom you don't know, making harmful accusations. Its downright scary.

Turning to our attention of the two suspects in custody.

Terri-Lynn Mcclintic, born on July 2 to a woman who was a stripper, who did not want to keep her child so we are told by media reports.

Mcclintic was relinquished to one Carol Mcclintic who so badly wanted a child that some sort of adoption took place.

We have heard from a variety of media reports that Terri-Lynn's childhood was not one of happiness, but one that was allegedly filled with abuse, which led her to moving to foster home to foster home, trying to find a sense of belonging. So according to the internet she led a very dark life, one of the secret fantasy of becoming a gang member, that would lead her to a path of destruction. One of Terri-Lynns passions was playing hockey and she was good according to the score records.

Although Terri-Lynn was arrested for the abduction & murder of Victoria Stafford, and its alleged that she was the unidentified women that picked Victoria up from school that day, is it true that it was her? Its been reported that the police think she is the one that did it, although many others looked like that police sketch as well as no one seemed to follow up on all the tips.

Could it be that she was so wanting a "Gangster" title, that she would confess to anything that the cops would tell her too. Or perhaps, she was just a scared teenager, that way over her head and guilty of nothing, but didn't know how to handle a group of law enforcement agencies interrogating her. Perhaps if she admitted anything it was because she was scared and felt that the only way to have the police stop questioning her was to tell them what they wanted to hear from her.

Or is it possible she was the women that abducted Victoria from her school One will have to wait for the trial to get the answers they seek with respect to what Terri-Lynn Mcclintic is guilty or not guilty of.

Unfortunately if the outcome is that she is innocent, many people are already out to get her according to threats posted on a variety of sites. Hopefully if she is innocent, that the truth will come out, and if she is guilty well there is no words for what punishment she should get.

Turning to Michael CS Thomas Rafertty, there was quite a lot of speculation about him, however, not very many details surrounding his childhood.

From his online presence it appeared he liked to hang out with the attractive women, he like name brand clothing, and liked living above his financial means. According to his online dating profiles on many dating sites, he had a difficult time finding Ms. Right. He claimed that he loved to dance, wasn't into game players, and took care of his body. He essentially was a ladies man.

Compiled from media reports, supposedly Michael, held a variety of jobs in the labor force, from working at a meat packaging plant to construction jobs.

Upon his arrest on May 19, 2009 for the Abduction & Murder of Victoria Stafford, Mr. Raferrty has been exercising his right to silence. Although many people would like to hear the version of events from him directly, so far he has not discussed it with anyone other than the lawyers that are representing him.

Although Michael Raferrty has not discussed anything, with the public, the general public convicted him as well online, based solely on his arrest, and the allegations of a relationship between himself and Terri-Lynn Mcclintic.

Forums were popping up on Facebook dedicated to making him and Terri-Lynn Mcclintic pay for the murder of Victoria Stafford. However, he has not been found guilty in a court of law. He had no previous criminal record, was not involved with drugs and his friends stated that he loves kids.

Now he was a marked man, and he could be very well innocent of such a crime. Many people tried to defend him, as there was huge speculation that he was just a pawn in this whole case, but every time people said anything, they were dumped on.

Perhaps it is good that Michael Rafertty is not discussing what happened, because from what we have seen so far, anyone that says anything on a forum, tends to get twisted.

Once the trial commences perhaps society will get the answers they thirst for. Somehow, its doubtful considering the conversation earlier with the detective, what if Michael is truly innocent and has been arrested for something he didn't do. How does he get back his life?

Of course no one will truly know what happened or if he had any involvement in the case until the trial, and even then the only people that truly know what happened is the people that were involved. As we all know that courtrooms are where lawyers and crown prosecutors present evidence of both sides, and then its up to the judge or a judge and jury to make a definitive answer of guilt based on the evidence provided.

Guilt or Innocence truly can only be proven in a court of law, or by eye witnesses who see the crime, and the perpetrator that commits that crime.

For sake of argument, how does Michael go back and live among a society that accused him of such a horrifying crime if he is found to be innocent. And what about all the speculations of him looking like the missing kid from Victoria BC 1991, named Michael Dunahee?

This is not the first time a player involved in this case has been accused of being a look alike to another child that has been abducted. Early on a women named Roselyn Knecht was accused of being the look alike of Tania Murrel, a girl that went missing from Edmonton Alberta, now Michael Rafertty is being accused of being a look alike of Michael Dunahee.

All of these variances of stories really makes it difficult for people to truly understand the complexity of the entire case.

This is a case of not only a murder and abduction of a beautiful girl, but it is also a case of false convictions. Although the outcome of the trial is far from being reached, people have already convicted Michael Rafertty, and Terri-Lynn Mcclintic as well as other people involved in the case. It goes to show how dangerous the internet can be. How just a few typed words and opinions of members of society can play an important role in such a serious case as this.

The internet played a very dangerous role in this case, at times it was helpful at other times it was dangerous to the investigation.

CHAPTER 8

"The Future"

Do you believe in psychics? What about the paranormal activity? Many people do not believe in psychics however, there is an equal amount of people who are believers.

The case of Victoria Stafford's abduction & murder seemed to have what some would call a psychic connection. Psychics were coming out of the woodwork from the very beginning. Whether or not the psychics that came out in the public eye were truly gifted with a psychic ability is truly up to you to decide. However, the psychics made many forecasts as to what happened.

It appeared that Ms. McDonald believed in the psychic phenomenon as well as when she took the alleged limo ride to Toronto she thought she was going to meet the Psychic Sylvia Brown. Even without a psychic connection, people are probably wondering what the outcome of this whole case is going to be.

Perhaps it will end with the two that are in custody found convicted, and that there were no other individuals involved in the crime.

As the case is still before the courts, the full story of what actually happened to Victoria Stafford, can't be told, however perhaps the horrifying details of what happened to her is better left untold.

Murders are never understood, more so when the victim is a child. A child that is innocent, and so full of life. How can someone take her away from all of those who loved her so much?

Hopefully, there will never be another murder, another missing child, or person but if there is lets just hope that people will think about what they post on the Worldwide Web.

Message from the Author

Dear Reader,

Writing this story was incredibly difficult due to the nature of the material. My purpose for writing this story wasn't to tell the story of "Victoria Stafford", but was to tell the story of how what we read on the Internet, Social Networking Sites such as Facebook, and what is presented to us by the Media leaves us an impression.

What we read, watch on television, allows us to form an opinion on a variety of issues. However, although we have an opinion, sometimes it is best to stay quiet and not inform others of it.

I myself formed an opinion of certain people in this case, although I continued to be an active voice with many of the sites mentioned in this book, I too was wrong to re-post things that I saw and that I read that there was no confirmation that the allegations had substance to them. And to that

I apologize. I too while researching the material for this book was personally attacked at writing such a book. Perhaps some people felt that as the story was not completed as of yet it should never have been written, or it should be written by the birthmother herself.

Some people wondered if it was a book of pure speculation, or if it had substance to it.

Now that you have read it for yourself what do you think.

Thank You for Reading

Dianna Holden

www.ingramcontent.com/pod-product-compliance
Lightning Source LLC
Chambersburg PA
CBHW051226050326
40689CB00007B/816